ROMANCING YOUR HUSBAND

DEBRA WHITE SMITH

HARVEST HOUSE PUBLISHERS
Eugene, Oregon 97402

Cover by Garborg Design Works, Minneapolis, Minnesota

Contributed material is used by permission.

ROMANCING YOUR HUSBAND
Copyright © 2002 by Debra White Smith
Published by Harvest House Publishers
Eugene, Oregon 97402
Library of Congress Cataloging-in-Publication Data

Smith, Debra White.
    Romancing your husband / Debra White Smith.
        p. cm.
    Includes bibliographical references.
    ISBN 0-7369-0606-1
    1. Christian women—Religious life. 2 Wives—Religious life. 3. Marriage—Religious aspects—Christianity. I. Title.

BV4527.S625 2002
248.8144—dc21   2001039430

Printed in the United States of America.

02 03 04 05 06 07 / BP-MS / 10 9 8 7 6 5 4 3 2 1

To my husband…

Daniel, we've been through a lot together. We've struggled together and grown up together. As we continue to mature as individuals and in our relationship, I want you to never forget that while my first goal is to please God, my second goal is to please you and do my best to make you blissfully happy.

Thanks for all our years in the past and thanks in advance for the years to come. You are my lover, my best friend, my hero, my confidante. I will love you forever!

Books by Debra White Smith

The Harder I Laugh, the Deeper I Hurt
(with Stan Toler; Beacon Hill Press)

SEVEN SISTERS SERIES
Second Chances

The Awakening

A Shelter in the Storm

To Rome with Love

For Your Heart Only

You may write to
Debra White Smith at:

P.O. Box 1482
Jacksonville, TX
75766

or

check out her website

www.debrawhitesmith.com

Contents

Foreword

DEBRA AND I HAVE BEEN MARRIED 20 YEARS NOW. We've had some bad times, but she's always been there for me. Because of that, I have never really been tempted to look at other women. I notice pretty faces, of course. What man doesn't? But there's always something that gives me the power to look away. I figure I've got the best at home, so why waste my time elsewhere?

The other day I was talking with some friends and the topic of sex came up. (Most of the time, husbands don't talk about their sex lives, but we are very good friends.) They basically said that after a while a husband can forget sex. I mentioned that I didn't have to worry about that because my wife takes care of me. They were all impressed. I didn't say much more, but I wondered if other wives know how important sex is to their husbands. A man who is satisfied feels like he can take on the world. A man who isn't loses confidence in himself as a man.

I'm just an average guy. I get up and go to work every day. I enjoy golf. In a lot of ways, I'm probably like your husband. I'm also crazy about my wife. When I see Debra, I smile and think about what she does for me. You may find some of her ideas challenging, but I encourage you to try them out. Your husband will love you for it...and you will reap the benefits. Please take it from a normal guy—what's written in this book is true. *It works!*

I love my wife a lot. The reason I think she's the best isn't because she's model perfect. I'm not either. It's because she puts all she has into fulfilling me. I never know what she's going to pull next to bring us closer together. And I like that. Life stays exciting when you live with a woman like that!

Daniel W. Smith

Ah, the Power of Love!

IMAGINE YOURSELF STANDING IN LINE to ride a wild and exhilarating roller coaster. Before you climb aboard, you notice a sign that says, "Brace yourself! This ride is full of twists, turns, and excitement!" That's exactly where you are right now—on the brink of an electrifying, unbelievable love affair with your husband! Whether you've been married 2 years, 20 years, or 40 years, your marriage can burn brighter and hotter if you implement the ideas and suggestions in this book.

You might say, "But, Debra, it's too late for my marriage." Don't be surprised by what God can and will do! He is in the business of mending the brokenhearted, setting captives free, and transforming bad relationships into dynamic havens of love, joy, and commitment. As you embark on this new adventure, you'll discover biblical principles and intriguing insights that can revolutionize your partnership.

And there's more! During this fantastic journey, there will come a moment when your husband will lovingly ask, "Now, what can I do for *you?*" When he does, hand him this book and tell him that chapters 2 and 4–8 are especially interesting. Are you thinking, "Debra, there's no way my husband will ever ask what he can do for me"? If you radically and fearlessly live what this book says, your husband will probably be so awed there's no telling what he'll do for you. If he doesn't read this book on your first request, don't despair. With ample doses of love, sweetness, and humility, wait until he asks again what he can do for you, then repeat your request that he read these chapters.

Remember, when you implement the concepts in this book, your marriage will most likely explode into the essence of unconditional love—a lifelong love that is the stuff dreams are made of. By that point, the two of you will be looking for ways to serve each other. Why am I so convinced? Because my marriage has done exactly that. And the truths in this book have been tested by more women than just me. The results have proven to be nothing short of miraculous! The journey may take some time, maybe a year or so, but hang in there even if dazzling love doesn't ignite overnight. Practicing these romance principles can turn your marriage into a taste of heaven on earth.

Are you ready? You are about to embark upon a fascinating, breathtaking journey...a journey that will transform your life and testify to a dying world that Christian marriages are the most thrilling on the planet!

In Christ's service,

Debra White Smith

1

"The Queen of Romance"

*So in everything, do to others
what you would have them do to you,
for this sums up the Law and the Prophets.*
MATTHEW 7:12

A LONG-TERM MARRIAGE RELATIONSHIP full of romance, excitement, and expectancy is a rare find. The typical couple usually meets, falls in love, gets married, and has a honeymoon for a couple of years—if they're fortunate. In the early years the romance is high and the fires burn at full flame. But the cares of life, the stress of having children, and the familiarity that grows from looking at the same spouse year in and year out can take its toll. Eventually, if a partner isn't willing to fan the flames of romance, the marriage relationship can and will grow stale. Romance will become almost nonexistent, and what used to be an electrifying sex life turns into a chore. Soon, what once was an enthused "Wow! It's you!" turns into a disenchanted groan and an "Oh, it's just you." The divorce rate in America reflects this plight. According to the National Center for Health Statistics, the divorce rate is 41 percent for first-time marriages.[1] Unfortunately the number of divorces for Christian marriages isn't that much different.

And that rate doesn't reflect the thousands of marriages that are legally together, but emotionally and physically divorced. Many couples are admired for staying together through the years, when in reality their relationship is either waning or kaput. They put on a happy face at church, but their marriage relationship long ago shriveled. You can forget romance! And sex is only an occasional occurrence. A wife might infrequently "give in," but the act is a duty just to keep her husband from annoying her.

When I had been married about seven years, a well-meaning friend told me, "Debra, after 15 years of marriage, you can forget the romance." Sadly, this claim is too often true. Another so-called nugget of wisdom I received states, "No matter how hot and steamy a relationship is at first, the passion will eventually die and there'd better be something to take its place." I firmly believe passion dies *only* if a husband and/or wife *allows* it to or a partner becomes so ill that romance takes a backseat to survival.

Despite all the open-mindedness about sex and the advancement of modern medicine, we still have a tendency to believe that exceptional, invigorating sex and romance happen only during the early stages of a relationship. Certainly there is an element of suspense and electricity when a couple is engaged and planning the wedding, and the electricity surges once the wedding vows are stated and the honeymoon begins. Those exhilarating, romantic days cannot be repeated in a relationship. Once they're over, they're over. Then it's time to move on to something longer lasting—the thrilling romance and physical relationship that a long-term commitment can achieve.

Most women who don't have an exciting marriage can easily tell you that the sexual issue boils down to a relationship issue. According to Gary Smalley in *Love Is a Decision,* women are relationship oriented: "Women have a built-in marriage manual....A wife is a gold mine of relational skills."[2] Women have a thermometer that constantly measures the status of our marital relationships. If our relationship is going well, then romance and sex will be excellent. If the relationship is not going well, then the romance dwindles and sex is anything but fulfilling.

In *His Needs, Her Needs,* Willard F. Harley Jr. states that while a woman's first need in a marriage is for affection, a man's first need is for sexual fulfillment.[3] Other research by Gary and Barbara

Rosberg claim that both the husband and wife's first need is for unconditional love, and their second needs are sexual for men, and emotional intimacy and communication for women.[4] Both findings prove that while women's top needs are emotional/relational, our husbands' top needs are physical/sexual. Harley further states that "when it comes to sex and affection, you can't have one without the other"[5] and "the typical wife doesn't understand her husband's deep need for sex any more than the typical husband understands his wife's deep need for affection."[6]

I have been married to the same man for 19 years, and I didn't need to read any books to figure out that my man needs sex. Furthermore, I've come to the conclusion that the difference between my husband's sex drive and mine is like the difference between a volcanic explosion and a small bundle of dynamite. From everything I have read and gleaned, I am a fairly amorous woman. But my husband, Daniel, has told me that I can take my most amorous moments, multiply them by two, and then I *might* understand exactly how he feels every other day of his life!

The bottom line? Men need sex…and women need affection, relationship, romance. We need to be adored, told we are beautiful, and shown open affection. We need candlelight dinners, clandestine getaways, and heartfelt conversation. Women enjoy romance.

Most women will tell you they wish their husbands were more romantic. Most men will tell you they wish their wives were more sexual. According to Harley, many men feel sexually cheated by their wives while many women feel emotionally cheated by their husbands.[7] It's very easy for a woman who feels emotionally cheated to focus on her husband's lack of fulfilling her needs and therefore stop meeting his sexual needs. Then, after a woman stops meeting her husband's sexual needs, a man certainly is not inclined to meet his wife's emotional needs for romance. And the cycle continues in a downward spiral until the marital relationship is nonexistent on all levels and a legal divorce has occurred—or an emotional and physical divorce has occurred while legally the marriage remains intact.

Recently a friend detailed a story about a young woman who said that during sex, she thought about what she needed to buy at the store. My friend told her, "You're going to *think* yourself right out of a husband." Well, she did. Being a Christlike wife is an equation that involves numerous aspects of home and family. Jesus Christ laid Himself down for others. If we are to be like Him, we will be willing to set aside our wants and meet the needs of our spouses. Even if your husband never divorces you, as did the above woman's, you can live year in and year out never holding your husband's heart and never experiencing the kind of heaven-on-earth marriage God intends for His children.

Do Unto Others

The Golden Rule tells us to treat other people the way we want to be treated in everything. That means all relationships and situations—including marriages. The gist of this involves laying down our rights and selflessly focusing on the needs of others. This type of love expects nothing in return and flows from a heart focused on the recipient of our actions. Furthermore, this love is active, not passive; positive, not negative. Before Jesus stated the Golden Rule in positive terms, others had voiced it in the negative:

- ♭ What is hateful to yourself do not do to someone else (Hillel, Jewish rabbi b. 60 B.C.).

- ♭ What you do not want done to yourself, do not do to others (Confucius, b. 551 B.C.).

- ♭ What you do not wish to be done to you, do not do to anyone else (Stoics, circa 300 B.C.).

Simply avoiding doing evil to others does not mean that a person is doing good. For instance, a woman can avoid doing evil to her husband while passively ignoring his needs and never doing him a favor. However, Jesus essentially said, "If you just don't do evil to others, you have only fulfilled half the mission. You must bend over backward to treat everyone else with as much love, respect, and dignity as you want to be treated." First Corinthians 13:4-8 defines this kind of selfless love: "Love is patient, love is kind. It does not envy, it does not boast, it is not proud. It is not rude, it is not self-seeking, it is not easily angered, it keeps no record of wrongs. Love does not delight in evil but rejoices with the truth. It always protects, always trusts, always hopes, always perseveres. Love never fails."

Exuding this type of love applies to *every* person, male and female, and *every* area of our lives, including issues of sex and romance in marriages. A primary way to put this type of selfless love into action is for wives to do everything in their power to understand their husbands' needs. Many women wrinkle their noses and complain that their husbands pester them about sex. "He has a one-track mind" is the cliché used to diagnose the masculine need for physical expression. However, I have never run across any studies that suggest men are born thinking, *Well, I may be only one day old, but when I grow up sex will be my number-one need.* Men don't plan or decide to need sex any more than women decide to need romance. When wives scorn their husbands' need for sex, they are neither living out the Golden Rule nor exemplifying selfless love. Furthermore, they are ridiculing them for a need God placed within them. Ultimately, this attitude represents disdain toward God and His creation. If we don't value our husbands' needs, they may also reflect the same attitude toward us concerning our needs for romance and affection.

"So in everything, do to others what you would have them do to you" (Matthew 7:12). This rule extends further than just our attitude toward our husbands' need for sex. The Golden Rule also applies to our *actions*. When your husband becomes amorous and makes erotic suggestions through touches or words, he is treating you the way he wants to be treated. He desperately wants you to desire him physically, and he puts much energy into assuring you that sex is what he wants by acting out his impulses. I have never heard of any man sitting back with folded arms and thinking, *I want sex, but she's going to have to come after me.* No! A husband lets his wife know what he wants—loudly and clearly—on a regular basis.

Well, that works for wives, too. If romance is what you need, then *you* pour romantic energies into your marriage. Instead of thinking, *Husband, romance me!* Why not do what your husband does regarding his needs—model your needs? This will change you from a woman who is yearning to be romanced into a woman who is finding fulfillment through romancing her husband. Pour as much energy into the romance of your relationship as your husband does into the sexuality of it. *You* sweep him away for a private weekend. *You* give him love notes. *You* make candlelit dinners just for him. I am not talking about planning something special once a year. Many people are able to do something romantic on their anniversaries and have a week or so of "warm fuzzies" for their spouses. I'm referring to building a *continual aura* of romance, excitement, and expectation into a marriage—regardless of how long you've been married. This kind of romance flows from unconditional love and gets deeper, richer, and more fulfilling as the years go by.

When I began romancing my husband—when I started acting out in our marriage what I wanted from him—our union went from good to extraordinary. Daniel and I had a solid marriage even before I turned into "the queen of romance." We had (and still have) our share of issues that needed to be worked through, and we did have moments of conflict. But, overall, we were both committed to each other. From what I've learned over time, our sex life was even a bit above average. Daniel was a caring husband and considerate about special occasions. However, my feelings of romantic fulfillment came and went until one day I realized I was expecting him to be a full-blown Romeo when I was being only half a Juliet: "My bounty is as boundless as the sea, My love as deep; the more I give to thee, The more I have, for both are infinite" (Juliet, in *Romeo and Juliet*, Shakespeare).

Let the Magic Begin

Juliet's claim of "the more I give to thee, the more I have" beautifully expresses the biblical concept of "give, and it will be given to you" found in Luke 6:38. Let's look at the total context of this verse: "Do not judge, and you will not be judged. Do not condemn, and you will not be condemned. Forgive, and you will be forgiven. Give, and it will be given to you. A good measure, pressed down, shaken together and running over, will be poured into your lap. For with the measure you use, it will be measured to you" (Luke 6:37,38). I've been involved in the church my whole life, and I have listened to numerous sermons on these powerful verses. While the principles of these verses apply to many areas of life, they also apply to the romance of a marriage.

If we stop judging and condemning our husbands for their need for sex and stop holding grudges from the past, we're free to use a big scoop and pour ample romance into our marriages. In turn, many husbands will respond romantically.

Proof This Works!

Our eighteenth Valentine's Day as a married couple was the best ever! Daniel called me the week before to ask me out on a date. I giggled and agreed. He even arranged for his mom to watch our children. I must say I was impressed! I had been putting a lot of energy into the romance of our marriage, and I was thrilled to see him responding in a like manner. Well, the day of our date arrived, and Daniel didn't feel well. He gradually grew sicker and sicker with an awful stomach virus. He worked outdoors at his mother's that day and came home ready to collapse. I told him we could wait until another night for our date, but he was insistent that we were going. However, he said he didn't have the energy to take the children to his mother's and also go on a date. I said that was fine. We could take the kids with us. Our children were the ripe old ages of three and five. Even though our date would be surrounded by a "cloud of witnesses," my heart was overflowing with respect and joy that my husband was thinking romantically.

When we got to the popular Mexican restaurant, I discovered he had made reservations. Wow! After we sat down, placed our order, and began munching on tortilla chips, four men approached our section. They were dressed alike in red vests, straw hats, and black slacks. I began sputtering, wondering if they were coming to our table. They stopped and handed me two roses. My eyes filled with tears. Daniel beamed. As the quartet started their a cappella serenade, everyone in the restaurant focused on our table. I was experiencing the most romantic and vitalizing Valentine present I have ever received. While the quartet sang "Heart of My Heart," "Let Me Call You Sweetheart," and "Sweet and Lovely," I alternated between watching them and looking at Daniel, whose eyes were glowing with love and honor. When the quartet finished, the whole restaurant clapped and cheered.

Never had Daniel been so secretive and so romantic. For me, this was proof that all the energy I had put into romancing him had indeed been responded to in overflowing measure. This wonderful serenade came from a man who had told me weeks before that he wasn't sure he knew how to be romantic. Heaven help me if he learns! I'll probably swoon with excitement! The irony of the whole evening was that by this point, I was eager to fulfill Daniel's every physical need, but he was so sick he went straight to bed when we got home. (This is real life, not a romance novel.) The next day, I had only one thing to say to him, "You just wait! I will *not* be outdone!" He smiled in anticipation.

A marriage with this kind of sparkle has a magical quality. Such thoughtfulness breeds adoration, respect, loads of love, and a "we can't keep our hands off each other" atmosphere. But only two hearts that are oozing love all over each other can make love—only two hearts that are striving to meet the other person's needs. This selflessness also revolutionizes sex, turning it into making love. When a wife is *making love,* she looks forward to the physical union. She doesn't want the intimate moments to end—and she might even cry when it's over because she's so happy. When a wife is *having sex,* she either dreads the physical union or is indifferent. She can't wait for it to be over and is relieved when she can go to sleep. Any husband and wife can have sex. It takes love, planning, and selflessness to create a lasting relationship that turns sex into the ultimate physical expression of love. This type of romance develops when husbands and wives are eager to live out Paul's message in 1 Corinthians 7:3-5: "The husband should fulfill his marital duty to his wife, and likewise the wife to her husband. The wife's body does not belong to her alone but also to her husband. In the same way, the husband's body does not belong to him alone but also to his wife. Do not deprive each other except by mutual consent."

> *Let him kiss me with the kisses of his mouth—*
> *for your love is more delightful than wine.*
> *Pleasing is the fragrance of your perfumes;*
> *your name is like perfume poured out.*
> *No wonder the maidens love you!*
> *Take me away with you—let us hurry!*
> *Let the king bring me into his chambers.*

SONG OF SONGS 1:2-4

Reality Checks

Personal

Being romantic can be a challenge when you're on the verge of a coma. There are occasions when I would rather roll over and snooze instead of meeting my husband's sexual needs. I have a five-year-old girl and a seven-year-old boy who, at times, run me ragged. Add to that an at-home writing career and speaking engagements, and I can assure you that I have been intimate with exhaustion.

Meeting the needs of our husbands is *a choice we make.* Living out the Golden Rule means viewing his sexual needs as a valuable part of who he is, not as a drudgery we have to endure. That means doing our best to fulfill our husbands' desires, even when we might not be in a particularly amorous mood. Anything less compromises selfless love. This doesn't mean there aren't nights when an exhausted spouse might ask for a rain check. But overall, the atmosphere of a Christlike marriage reveals a wife and a husband who make sure the other is physically satisfied.

Communication

Communication is essential to any situation, including the romance of a marriage. *Regularly and lovingly sharing your emotional needs* for romance and affection while acting out your needs will eventually communicate your message. When I say "regularly," I'm referring to being open to the leading of the Holy Spirit and discussing the subject as it naturally arises. It might take discussing the issue three times a year for two years before the message is clearly heard and understood. When I say "lovingly," I mean with a considerate and caring spirit, not with a tone of accusation. (See chapters 4 and 5.) Ask your husband to read Gary Smalley's *Love Is a Decision* (Word), Willard F. Harley Jr.'s *His Needs, Her Needs* (Revell), and anything by Les and Leslie Parrott (Beacon Hill Press; Zondervan). If he won't read these, then lovingly share tidbits from them or snippets from this book as the opportunity arises. The more eager you are to meet your husband's needs, the more likely he will be to heed your input.

If your marriage is in severe straits, a Christian counselor can assist in the communication process. Be careful. Make sure the counselor has an excellent reputation and will *pray* with you instead of only offering advice. Just because someone hangs "Christian Counselor" on his or her door does not mean you will receive biblical truth. Unwise or antibiblical counsel, even from a Christian, will heap problems on top of problems. If your husband will not go to a counselor, continue to intercede for him in prayer. Allow God to begin carving you into His image. The more you submit to the purging of the Lord, the better wife you will be and the more willing your husband will be to listen to you—on all subjects.

Physical

A woman's sexual desire fluctuates. As a young woman, physical desires vary according to the menstrual cycle. After menopause, the desire may almost cease. Or you may be a woman who naturally has a low libido. If you find yourself struggling to physically respond to your husband, I recommend reading *Intimate Issues: 21 Questions Christian Women Ask About Sex* by Linda Dillow and Lorraine Pintus (Waterbrook, 1999). Also, check with your doctor regarding medications, supplements, and key physical exercises that may increase your desire.

While physical problems do exist, I have found that often they are compounded by the choices women make. If a woman spends mental time degrading romance and the physical union, she will be less inclined to desire physical expressions of love. However, if a woman envisions herself and her husband engaged in intimacy and uses mental energy to plan romantic encounters, then physical responses naturally follow.

Prayer Points for Romance

If the romance in your marriage is nominal or nonexistent, the following prayer points are crucial to breathing the life back into your marriage. I recommend them as a part of your daily devotions.

- Pray that God will renew and empower your love for your husband.

- Pray that God will increase your sexual desire for your husband.

- Pray that you will be more interested in meeting your husband's needs than your own.

- Pray that the Lord will give you patience with yourself and your spouse in your journey to spectacular romance.

- Ask the Lord to show you creative and exciting ways to romance your husband.

Romantic Notions

Who is this that appears like the dawn, fair as the moon,
bright as the sun, majestic as the stars in procession?"

SONG OF SONGS 6:10

What I Did

For our sixteenth anniversary, I planned a secret getaway to a bed-and-breakfast(B&B) in a nearby town. This place looks like it came straight out of the pages of a Victorian magazine. I packed our bags and composed a sensuous, romantic note that I taped to the steering wheel in Daniel's car while he was at work. In the note I told him he was being kidnapped, and that *I* was his anniversary present. I promised a weekend of enchantment and gave him a map and written directions to the bed-and-breakfast. I went to the B&B, changed into some red lingerie, and waited for him near the front door. Because our anniversary is the week before Christmas, we had the whole B&B to ourselves.

My Reason

This was my husband's introduction to the new, romantic me. I had decided the time had come to stop waiting and wishing for him to be more romantic and to start being romantic myself. I wanted to blow his socks off with a weekend he would never forget.

How I Felt

I was so excited I could hardly contain myself. Daniel knew I had already "bought" his anniversary present and one evening he asked, "Is this something we can both use?" I almost burst into hilarious laughter. Later I learned he thought I had bought a new office chair for our computer desk. How boring! Along with being excited about the weekend, I was also exhausted from trying to juggle the getaway with a two-year-old and four-year-old hanging on to my skirts.

The Obstacles I Overcame

My main obstacles were trying to go to the store for new lingerie and some sparkling grape juice, get my husband and me both packed, and get my children to a friend's house, all before four o'clock in the afternoon. This doesn't sound like much, but we had adopted our Vietnamese daughter, who was two at the time, and had only had her about six months. Pulling her from the orphanage deeply disturbed her, and she screamed for almost two years after we got her. The whole time I was preparing to leave, Brooke was following me around the house, screaming as if she were being attacked.

My Husband's Response

Daniel had left 16 red roses along with my anniversary gift on the dining room table. He called midday to see if I had noticed the roses. Brooke was screaming, Brett (4) wanted my undivided attention, and I was sleep deprived and exhausted. I said, "Yes, I see the roses. I know they're in there, but I can't go get them right now." I bid him a harassed, quick goodbye and hung up. Later on, Daniel told me that after he hung up, he got really aggravated. He told one of his coworkers that he had gone to a lot of trouble for our anniversary, and I didn't act like I cared one bit. This is the frame of mind in which he read my note on the steering wheel. After reading the note, he said he was dumbfounded and thought, *I have been outdone.* He arrived at the bed-and-breakfast in a state of awe. Since we were the only people on the premises, I gave Daniel a tour of the whole B&B. (Yes—I was dressed in my new lingerie to add a festiveness to the tour!) He kept saying, "This place is gorgeous." Then he would chuckle and say, "I have been outdone."

What I Wish I Had Done

I planned our initial intimate encounter for before dinner. I should have waited until after dinner. We were both starving and tired. I think a time of relaxation, food, and emotional intimacy would have made our physical union sparkle a bit more.

Budget Suggestions

The budget for this one night getaway was about $130, including meals and inexpensive lingerie. One of the things I did to make the weekend more economical was to arrange to trade babysitting with a trusted friend instead of paying a sitter. If you don't have funds for a bed-and-breakfast, you can always create your own at home. Spruce up your bed with netting on the posts, light candles, prepare a fancy meal, play romantic music...use your imagination.

Special Note

Are you inspired and want to begin romancing your husband today? If so, feel free to check out chapter 9 for more exciting encounter ideas!

2

A More Excellent Way

And yet I show you a more excellent way.
1 CORINTHIANS 12:31, NKJV

The Cows Are Out

AT ONE TIME, MY HUSBAND AND I OWNED a home out in the boondocks. Our small, brick house was the epitome of country living with a stylish interior and expansive yard. It was located down a winding country lane surrounded by pastures, trees, and even had a beaver pond at the back of the five-acre plot. We had only one neighbor that we could see and several who were out of sight.

That close neighbor owned cattle that she kept in a pasture down the road. One morning I was awakened by the sounds of crunching, munching, and mooing—that sounded way too close. I peeked out the front window to see my yard full of huge horned beasts that acted as if they were setting up permanent residence. Immediately, I called my neighbor-in-sight, Joyce, and inquired whether the cattle belonged to her and her husband. After my description, she determined that the cattle did belong to them. By this point, the moo-moos were meandering around my yard and on the road.

I hung up the phone, and the next thing I knew an attractive, 40-something woman—with her hair curled and her lipstick firmly in place—was riding down the road on a four-wheeler screaming, "Yah, yah, get on home, cows! Yah, Yah!" The cows lowered their ears and started trotting up the road, back to their designated pasture.

Joyce and her four-wheeler successfully corralled every one of those cattle. She temporarily fixed the broken-down fence so they couldn't escape again. Later, she and her husband worked together to permanently repair the fence.

But what would have happened if, when I called Joyce, she sat back, crossed her arms, and said, "I'm not going to chase down those cows. That's my husband's role. God has ordained him as the manager of our cattle—not me." Well, I will tell you what would have happened. Those cows, worth a year's salary, would have wandered around all day. Some of them might have gotten lost while another one or two might have been slaughtered on the road by an unsuspecting driver. In short, the humorous fiasco could have turned into a huge financial loss.

> *The art of love is largely the art of persistence.*
> ALBERT ELLIS

Sometimes marriages are a lot like the cow fiasco. There are times when the marital fences need to be mended, but we have become so preoccupied with who's supposed to do what that we fold our arms, step back, and refuse to fix the problem. *Our marriages are our most treasured possessions!* The time has come for Christian wives to lay aside the assumption that female passivity is godly. If we sit back, fold our arms, and say, "I cannot take any initiative in any aspect of my marriage because I will be trespassing God's law of marital norms," then we might as well let $50,000 worth of cattle wander around all day and never lift a finger to fix the problem. Perhaps we have defined our marital roles to the point that we have tied our own hands.

You can go to a Christian bookstore and find books that will analyze Scripture in just about every way imaginable. Christian authors have delved into the Greek and Hebrew. They've analyzed the King James Version, New International Version, and more.

Our pile of reference books present a number of viewpoints along a wide range of denominational interpretations. Every theory is supposedly supported by Scripture, despite the fact that some of them contradict each other. Some hypotheses are formulated by people who have been married awhile and some by those who have never made that commitment.

I don't mind analyses. I have a tendency toward analytical thinking myself. (At times I figure I could analyze my way out of a cavern on the back side of Siberia. Sometimes my husband's interpretation of my analytical thinking is, "You would argue with a fence post.") But at times I think in all our arguing and proving and role defining, we have missed the point of what God did in the Garden of Eden when He created two people to love each other, complement each other, and live together in harmony. Jesus was a great one to speak up when people missed the point. When the Jewish leaders asked Him about divorce, He essentially said, "Remember the Garden of Eden? You missed the point" (Matthew 19:8). When the disciples wanted to know who was the greatest, He reached for a child and said, "You missed the point" (Matthew 18:1-4). When He healed the man's hand on the Sabbath, the Pharisees challenged His audacity to work on Sunday. Jesus looked at them and, in effect, said, "Shouldn't I do good on the Sabbath? You've missed the whole point!" (Mark 3:1-6). And when Christ stretched out His arms and died on the cross, He said, "Father, forgive them; they missed the point" (paraphrase of Luke 23:34).

Likewise, we can become so preoccupied with who is supposed to do what in a marriage that we can miss the point. Instead of a husband and wife sailing the seas of life in the same boat, rowing *together,* trimming the sails *together,* and making sure the whole operation runs smoothly *together,* many spouses are actually in two different boats! Yet the two won't truly become one until they *do* get into the same boat.

Since my husband and I got into the same boat, there have been times when we had revealing communication about the roles in our marriage. This usually involves his wrapping his arms around me and saying something to the effect, "What can I do to make your life better?" I respond with, "No, let me make your life better. Is there anything I can do to help you at all?" He replies with something like, "I asked first. It's my turn to serve you." The hug lengthens, grows warmer, and a cloud of love descends upon us.

My husband and I are two ordinary people who live in a small town in Texas. We have two young children who are normal (if the toys strewn all over the den are valid proof). We have four adult cats, one of which just gave birth to five kittens. We own two parakeets that my husband is threatening to fry for dinner. This morning I left the beds unmade, dishes in the sink, and laundry undone. We go to church three times a week and Wal-Mart about five times a week. Both of us were raised in small, doctrinally mainstream churches, with an attendance of 60 on a good Sunday. We came from hardworking families with a decided absence of generational fortune. Even though we have both sat on a few jets, neither of us would qualify as jet-setters, and we never will fit into that crowd. In many ways, our lives are just like millions of Christian couples all over the U.S.

With one exception. After almost two decades together, we have a to-die-for marriage. We have the kind of union many women lie awake at night and yearn to have. Daniel and I are best friends and lovers. We can't get enough of each other. We think the same things are funny and laugh at each other's jokes—even when nobody else does. We admire each other's strengths and try to minimize our weaknesses. We've each put the other on a pedestal and are convinced that there's not another human being in the world that compares. I'd rather be with my husband than anyone. As Shakespeare says, "We are such stuff as dreams are made on"; as God says, "The two become one person" (Genesis 2:24 TLB).

Through the years I have listened to numerous well-meaning experts—some married, some not—eloquently deliver sermons or presentations on what the marriage roles are and what it takes to have an excellent marriage. And in all my years of interacting around the church and observing people up close, I have seen precious few marriages that have a spirit of "two hearts melting all over each other," that echo the refrain "I'm nuts about you," and that strive to maintain the goal of "making you look good, making you a success, making you feel like the most important person on the planet."

These are the goals of an excellent marriage. According to Lawrence Richards, reflecting on Ephesians 5, "Paul is not speaking about the institution of marriage, but about the relationship of marriage partners. When the husband loves with Christ's love, and with Christ's intent, and cares as much for his wife's well-being as he does his own, the issues so often debated are easily resolved."[1] Likewise, God calls for everyone, including wives, to fulfill Ephesians 5:1,2: "Be imitators of God, therefore, as dearly loved children and live a life of love, just as Christ loved us and gave himself up for us as a fragrant offering and sacrifice to God." A wife who reveres and loves her husband on this level soon learns that many problems cease to exist. The spirit of a marriage is not about cookie-cutter role definitions, it's about sacrificial, unconditional love from both spouses.

> *And yet I show you a more excellent way. Though I speak with the tongues of men and of angels, but have not love, I have become sounding brass or a clanging cymbal. And though I have the gift of prophecy, and understand all mysteries and all knowledge, and though I have all faith, so that I could remove mountains, but have not love, I am nothing. And though I bestow all my goods to feed the poor, and though I*

*give my body to be burned, but have not love, it
profits me nothing. Love suffers long and is kind; love
does not envy; love does not parade itself, is not puffed
up; does not behave rudely, does not seek its own, is
not provoked, thinks no evil; does not rejoice in iniq-
uity, but rejoices in the truth; bears all things, believes
all things, hopes all things, endures all things. Love
never fails. But whether there are prophecies, they
will fail; whether there are tongues, they will cease;
whether there is knowledge, it will vanish away. For
we know in part and we prophesy in part. But when
that which is perfect has come, then that which is in
part will be done away. When I was a child, I spoke as
a child, I understood as a child, I thought as a child;
but when I became a man, I put away childish things.
For now we see in a mirror, dimly, but then face to
face. Now I know in part, but then I shall know just
as I also am known. And now abide faith, hope, love,
these three;* but the greatest of these is love.

1 CORINTHIANS 12:31–13:13
NKJV, emphasis added

Sacred Romance

Ironically, the means to a love-drenched marriage is to release
the idea that a man can be your "everything." At any given
moment, you can turn on the radio and hear a host of singers
with varying styles proclaim that another living person is his or
her reason for living. American greeting cards declare "I can't live
without you." The messages that a woman can fall in love in two
weeks and that a man will be her ultimate fulfillment permeates
our culture. Movies insinuate the same. In his book *Romantic
Love*, James Dobson asserts that we have a preoccupation in
America with such erroneous concepts as love at first sight.[2]

While I do believe that a person in tune with the Lord can have a certain knowing that he or she has met that special someone, we fool ourselves if we think we can plumb the depths of mature love within a short, initial meeting. Deep, true love doesn't happen overnight. Neither does mature romance. Those things happen when each person makes *Jesus Christ* his or her reason for living, not the potential spouse. Real love—the kind that burns strong through the decades—comes as a direct result of a sacred romance with Jesus.

When women stop focusing on their husbands as the only means of filling the emptiness in their souls and start focusing on Jesus Christ, a new love springs forth. A special love. A love that doesn't wane even in the face of conflict or a husband's imperfections. This love comes straight from the heart of God and permeates the marriage with a honeylike glow. No human being is capable of this kind of selfless love; it only comes through the Lord. It fully matures after a woman has spent hours a week, month in and month out, allowing the Lord to purify her heart and carve her into His image.

> Do you want to know Christ as your personal Savior? Believe that Jesus Christ is the Son of God, is actually God in the flesh. Confess that you are a sinner and that you need His forgiveness for your sins. Ask Christ to forgive you for all the wrong you've done. Find a Bible and begin reading the New Testament—starting with the book of Matthew. Join a Bible-based church. Share your new faith with your husband. If he doesn't immediately believe, don't push him. Pray for him daily.

No marriage can have true intimacy until we are willing to allow God total access to our hearts. If a woman is resisting the Lord and refuses to develop intimacy with the force that created her, then she will likewise never experience that melting-all-over-each-other intimacy with her husband. If we keep out God, then we will inadvertently keep out our mates. Only after we relinquish every fiber of our being to the Lord are we capable of being a conduit of the selfless kind of love that being a godly spouse is all about.

Heightened marital romance only occurs after deep intimacy and romance with God has been achieved. God becomes the force upon which our being is centered. This allows our husbands freedom to be themselves, to simply be human beings, to be free of the pressure of wives who believe their mates should be perfect. Releasing our all to the Lord allows us to sacrificially love our husbands the way they are, without that "need" to change them.

However, just because a woman is a Christian and attends church does not guarantee that she is truly intimate with Jesus Christ. Just because a woman is entering her mature years, there is no guarantee that she has or has ever had a powerful relationship with the Lord. I travel and speak all over the United States, and often women approach me with their problems. No matter what the problem, one of my solutions remains the same: Spend time with God every day—if not every day, at least several times a week. Plug in that worship music, plop onto your couch, close your eyes, and sit in His presence for at least 30 minutes to an hour a day. Don't ask Him for a thing. Don't request that He change your husband or anybody else. Don't dictate to God how you think He should answer your prayers. Simply turn your heart toward Him, think about Him, and ask Him to permeate your being, to carve you into His image, to show you how to love your husband. Psalm 46:10 says it best: "Be still, and know that I am God." There's a direct connection between knowing God and being still. The inverse is that if you aren't still you won't know Him. After you have spent time in worship, soaking Him up, *then* bring your requests to Him. After request time, I usually read my Bible. And in the presence of the God that created me, the Bible leaps to life and ministers to me in a dynamic, life-changing way.

A divine intimacy develops through regularly absorbing the presence of God. From that supernatural romance, God's power will flow through you and supercharge your marriage with a love straight from heaven. Not only will your marriage be revolution-ized, but every relationship you have will benefit from God's unconditional love oozing from you.

Perhaps you're thinking, *That's exactly what I need because right now I don't love my husband in the least.* I must respond by being transparent. My husband and I haven't always had the kind of marriage we now have. We got married when I had just turned 19 and my husband was about two weeks from 23. I often say that the beauty of getting married young is that you get to grow up together, and those youthful years spent as one hold the potential for forming a strong lifelong bond. The drawback of getting mar-ried so young is all the upheaval a couple can put each other through during the maturation process. My husband and I have both needed to exercise ample doses of forgiveness and plenty of love in order to survive those turbulent, youthful years. Only in the last few years have we looked at each other and said, "Oh! So this is real love! Were we in love before?" Certainly we experienced the normal giddiness and new love during our courtship and early marriage. I even knew when I met Daniel—I was 15 and he was 19—that there was something special about him, that perhaps he might be my lifelong mate. However, there's a depth of love that a long-term marriage can experience that makes the early years seem shallow and capricious. Sadly, there are many couples who stay together 50 years and never recover from the wounds inflicted during the youthful struggles of early marriage. Sometimes I wonder if my husband and I would have been trapped in the pain of the past had I not started seeking God with my whole heart as Psalm 42:1,2 pictures: "As the deer pants for streams of water, so my soul pants for you, O God. My soul thirsts for God, for the living God. When can I go and meet with God?"

A significant element in the health of my marriage lay within me. The more I panted after and sought God, the stronger I became spiritually. The more I allowed God to change me, the less I focused on my husband's flaws, and the quicker my marriage grew into the powerful relationship Daniel and I share. The transformation took several years of intense spiritual work, but it was worth the effort! This pursuit of the holy and of God's love is indeed "a more excellent way." Amazing, isn't it, that a woman can hold that much God-ordained power? As Gary Smalley says, women really are the relationship monitors of their marriages. You have a *major* impact on the spirit of love in your marriage!

> *We need to find God,*
> *and he cannot be found in noise and restlessness.*
> *God is the friend of silence.*
> *See how nature—trees, flowers, grass—*
> *grows in silence; see the stars, the moon and the sun,*
> *how they move in silence....*
> *We need silence to be able to touch souls.*
>
> MOTHER TERESA

Reality Checks

Personal

My husband and I have a joke. He says that all this "romancing your husband" business sounds really good...unless he tries to romance me on Sunday afternoon or at 6:00 A.M. We all have our limits. Honestly, I'm not ready to melt all over anything but my pillow during those hours. My Sunday afternoon nap borders on being sacred. And at 6:00 A.M. I usually feel like somebody has hit me over the head with a baseball bat. I don't normally grasp what day of the week it is, what month of the year, or what my name is at that time. Therefore, I often suspiciously scrutinize the strange man wandering down the hallway. He might *claim* to be my husband, but a woman just can't be too careful! All this is to say that when I talk about a spirit of encompassing the other in love, I am referring to the general spirit of the marriage. There are times in every marriage when heightened romance or thoughts of love aren't an option—during childbirth, a bout with a stomach virus, or after a four-year-old floods the bathroom, for example. When these crises are over, however, then the love response springs forth, glowing with unconditional love, acceptance, and a heavy dose of God's grace.

Time

Yes, it takes time to romance the Lord *and* your husband. Regardless of your constraints, I encourage you to commit time and energy to your relationship with them. For instance, what this means for me is that I seldom watch television. The only time I watch it is if it offers a bonding opportunity with me and my children or my husband. My children have a favorite afternoon show that we sit down and enjoy together. My husband and I often enjoy a movie if we're on a stay-at-home date. But I have no favorite shows and no television schedule. My time priorities are my marriage and my God. (I figure I can regularly watch television if I ever end up at a nursing home.)

Another hard choice I've made is to limit e-mail to necessary interpersonal interaction or business-related issues. If you have surfed the net lately, you probably have realized that it, too, can take up your whole life. E-mail and the internet can be so addictive. God has shown me that I have no business devoting family and/or spouse time to computer pursuits. Modern inventions are great. I have a website myself. But avoid letting this modern convenience consume your life.

Another time management choice I made was hiring a housekeeper. There was a time when I couldn't afford help, so I understand if you can't right now. However, I would rather drive a used vehicle and have a housekeeper than buy a new vehicle every couple of years. Having a housekeeper, even once or twice a month, frees you from being strapped by so many domestic duties. If your husband balks at the idea, explain to him that a housekeeper means more romance for him. Most men will be supportive on those terms! (My husband was just thrilled to see a clean house for a change. Forget the romance—he was just glad to see the floor!) Another option is to involve the whole family in household chores.

These are just a few time choices from my life. Perhaps there are other areas in your life where you can juggle your time to develop deeper relationships with the Lord and your husband. I have found that the Lord is faithful in helping me manage my time more wisely.

Spiritual

I would love to tell you that I never fail in having my daily devotions, but I cannot. There are some weeks when I struggle to get alone with God twice. I believe most mothers of small children would attest to the same. But overall, I average a powerful prayer time about four or five times a week; there are weeks when I don't miss a day. Even though I am having the time of my life romancing my husband, chasing after my kids, writing, and speaking, I sometimes fantasize about the years when I will have more hours in my day to devote to absorbing the presence of God. But even the time I spend with the Lord now transforms me, empowers me to live according to the Word of God, and infuses my marriage with love.

If you don't have a meaningful prayer life, start today! We are all busy. There will always be a reason not to pray and read your Bible. But saying we are too busy to spend time alone with God is the physical equivalent of saying we are too busy to take a bath. My time with God keeps my heart pure, my mind focused, and my attitudes squeaky clean before my Lord.

Prayer Points for Sacred Romance

If you are struggling with developing a potent devotional life, the following suggestions will empower you to seek God with all your heart.

- If you believe you must be weak spiritually because you are female, pray that the Lord will overturn that erroneous thought process.

- Pray that the Lord will give you the strength to listen when He calls you to act. Be open to prayer at odd hours if that is the only way you can work in a quiet time. (After we adopted our daughter, I was often awake at night with her, so my prayer time would happen at 2 or 3 A.M.)

- Pray that God will bring stability to your devotional time.

- Ask the Lord to make His Word spring to life for you. (Reading the books of Esther and Ruth are great places to start.)

- Pray that God will give you the courage to obey Him when He begins the cycle of purging and blessing in your heart. Don't be surprised if God impresses you through thoughts and Scripture to make some form of restitution with your husband—even in an area where your husband might have been at fault first. A husband's initial sin does not justify his wife's responding with a sinful attitude…and vice versa. If you do not heed the Lord, your marriage and spiritual growth will be stunted.

Romantic Notions

Entreat me not to leave you, or to turn back from following after you; for wherever you go, I will go; and wherever you lodge, I will lodge; your people shall be my people, and your God, my God. Where you die, I will die, and there will I be buried. The LORD do so to me, and more also, if anything but death parts you and me.

RUTH 1:16,17 NKJV

What I Did

I arranged for Daniel and me to restate our wedding vows. In the past, any time I had thought of doing this I envisioned an entire wedding. Me in a tea-length gown; my husband in a tuxedo. The candles. The bridesmaids. The flowers. The reception. Something of that magnitude would be almost impossible to pull off with a household to run, two small children to take care of, book deadlines, and speaking engagements. Then one day, I thought, *Why do I have to recreate a full-blown wedding? Why can't I just have a simple, surprise ceremony?* So that's what I did. I called the preacher who wed us (he is now retired) and had him meet us at our small church. No decorations. No guests. No hoopla. Just Daniel and me and the minister and his wife. This was a total surprise to Daniel.

My Reason

This was our eighteenth anniversary, and I wanted to do something really special. In preceding years we had been able to get away overnight by ourselves, but this year that wasn't possible. Therefore, I wanted to do something that would be as exciting as a clandestine getaway. Also, our love had deepened during that year to the point that we were both dizzy with it all. I wanted a ceremony of renewed commitment that would represent our thriving love.

How I Felt

The day of the ceremony, I was giddy. Daniel knew I had something special planned, but he didn't have a clue about what it could be. I must also admit I was a little smug. I knew I had come up with something better than his having me serenaded in the restaurant on Valentine's Day. I was indeed fulfilling my claim that I would not be outdone!

Obstacles to Overcome

A couple of weeks before the ceremony, I almost backed out. I started thinking that perhaps it wouldn't work or maybe it wouldn't be all that special. My main obstacle was my own mental hesitations.

My Husband's Response

I had Daniel drive to the church, and we got out of the van. I stopped outside the church door, held his hands, and said, "Now, I've got a question. Will you marry me?" By this point, he was smiling big. He said yes! We walked down the aisle arm in arm. The minister was already awaiting us. By this point, there was electricity sparking between us.

The ceremony turned out to be about 100 times more meaningful than our original wedding. We both cried when we vowed our undying love "until death do us part." This time, we had a more mature understanding of the concept of marriage. The years we had already spent together sweetened the moment. After the brief ceremony, we went out to eat. Daniel said, "Well, you did it! You outdid me." I smiled smugly. Then he said, "But I've got plans that are even better than this!"

What I Wish I Had Done

I asked my pastor's wife to put on a special CD of love songs. She chose some saxophone music. The idea was a good one and the music was great, but I turned it up too loud. I should have kept the music barely discernible. The melodies were a little distracting.

Budget Suggestions

I paid the minister $25 for the approximate hour we took out of his day, which allotted for travel time, putting on a suit, and so on. He really didn't want to be paid because we're good friends. However, I insisted. I didn't buy any new clothes—just wore dressy, casual slacks. You can spend about as much or little as you like on this romantic interlude.

3
Space and Grace

When I was a child, I talked like a child, I thought like a
child, I reasoned like a child. When I became a man,
I put childish ways behind me.
1 CORINTHIANS 13:11

Definition of Outdoor Barbecuing

BBQ IS USUALLY THE ONLY TYPE OF COOKING a "real" man will do.
When a man volunteers to do such cooking, the following chain
of events is put into motion:

1. The woman goes to the store to buy all the ingredients
   for the meal.

2. The woman fixes the salad, vegetables, and dessert.

3. The woman prepares the meat for cooking, places it on a
   tray along with the necessary cooking utensils, and takes
   it to the man, who is lounging beside the grill, drinking a
   cola.

4. The man places the meat on the grill.

5. The woman goes inside to set the table, put out the condi-
   ments, and check the vegetables.

6. The woman comes out to tell the man the meat is
   burning.

7. The man gets off his lounge chair, puts his cola down,
   takes the meat off the grill, and hands it to the woman.

8. The woman prepares the plates and brings them to the table.

9. After eating, the woman clears the table and does the dishes.

10. The man asks the woman how she enjoyed "her night off." And, upon seeing her annoyed reaction, concludes that there's just no pleasing some women.[1]

Who's the Mother?

In some households, the barbecue scenario is closer to truth than many are comfortable admitting. One complaint I often hear from women is, "My husband is helpless. The poor guy can't do anything for himself." What astounds me is that these "helpless men" often run or manage corporations, pastor a church, maneuver major machinery, or orchestrate brain surgery. But when they come through the front door of their own home, it's like they set aside the man and put on a child who needs to be cared for. What an interesting cycle of independence and dependency. After much thought, I've come to the conclusion that helpless men are not born—they are made. Many times the women who complain about their husbands' inability to function in the home are the ones who take over every job their men try to do. For instance, if a husband attempts to dress the children, the wife is right there, fussing about how it isn't done right and changing everything from shoes to hair bows. If he unloads the dishwasher, the woman gripes because he didn't put the bowls and cups in the "right" place. If he attempts to cook dinner, the woman breaks in and starts stirring the peas because they are about to burn. Next, she begins hurling orders in an attempt to get this near disaster "under control." If the man tries to do the laundry, the woman fumes for a week because he washed a fuzzy towel with her skirt. And he never gets the towels folded correctly. Or maybe the woman doesn't verbalize her complaints. Maybe she just silently takes over and shoos him out of the kitchen or laundry room or flowerbed.

What happens next is amazing. Most adult males, when faced with such actions, simply withdraw. They stop trying to help. When the wife winds up doing everything, she resents it. The wife thinks, *What kind of man would blissfully sit in a recliner and watch TV while his wife works like a horse?* Once the respect is gone, then the marriage might as well be gone, too. And romance? Instead of the bedroom sizzling, it barely warms up.

Here's a fascinating fact: Many men are perfectly capable of living by themselves and taking care of any and all domestic needs in one fashion or another. And a lot of them did this before they got married! For instance, when "helpless husbands" lived alone, ironing was a simple task. Many smart men learned that if they laid their slacks flat under the mattress the night before, the pants came out looking partially ironed. No, they weren't perfect, but they were presentable. But in many households, if a married man tries something like this, his wife turns into a mother figure who fusses and insists that she "do it right."

When a woman stops being her husband's wife and starts being his mother, the marriage is nowhere near what God intended. Healthy males are looking for a lover, a companion, a partner, a loyal friend—not a mother. Many reasonable men are willing to assist with the domestic duties if they are given ample room to fail and plenty of space and grace to grow.

I cannot count the number of times I have had women observe my marriage then say, "You don't know how lucky you are! Daniel does so much with the kids and around your house. My husband would *never* do that much." I usually just smile and say something like, "Yes, he is a phenomenal man, isn't he?" But really, my husband's sense of household responsibility has precious little to do with luck. It has everything to do with my giving him the *space and grace* to assist in any way he can and never trying to "fix" what he has done. In recent weeks…

    ♭ *I have gone to church then noticed my little girl's dress was on backwards—not once, but twice.* My husband dressed her. I say, "Praise the Lord! The man took initiative in dressing his daughter." And not once did I complain.

    ♭ *I have gone to church with my little boy's shirt looking a bit rumpled because it needed to be ironed before my husband dressed him.* Before leaving for church, I commented, "Does Brett's shirt need to be ironed?" Daniel said, "No, I thought it looked okay." I examined it and was sorely tempted to take if off Brett, slap it on the ironing board, and press away. Instead, I shrugged and said, "Yeah, I think it's okay." And it really was!

    ♭ *I have observed my husband dump two pounds of half-cooked hamburger patties on the ground while trying to use our new grill.* I could have barged in and said, "Let me do that! You can't do anything right." Or I could have made cutting remarks about his ineptitude. Instead, I shrugged and gave him more meat. (My innumerable cats enjoyed the feast!)

    ♭ *I have repeatedly watched as mounds of garbage pile up before he takes it to the curb.* I could fume and nag and take out the garbage myself. Instead, I figure it's just garbage and the whole thing won't matter in a hundred years anyway. I repeatedly conclude that when he gets tired of it stacking up, he'll do something about it. He always does!

    ♭ *I have found my little girl's clothes all neatly folded on the air hockey table in my little boy's room.* I could have griped because Daniel didn't put the clothes in her room or in her dresser, but I didn't. I thought, *Well, praise the Lord! My husband folded clothes!* Eventually, I moved the clothes to my little girl's room. But for a while, they were really handy on that air hockey table.

Many helpless men are not born. They are made! Sometimes, but not always, the mothers begin the scenario and the wife picks up where the mother left off. The remedy is that the mother-wife needs to step back, stop treating her husband like a child, and allow him to be a *man*. Give your husband the freedom to fulfill 1 Corinthians 13:11, "When I was a child, I talked like a child, I thought like a child, I reasoned like a child. When I became a man, I put childish ways behind me."

I believe that when a wife enables a man to be completely dependent upon her in a childlike fashion, she gains an element of power over him. Instead of being a healthy, interdependent relationship, the marriage turns into a dependency where one spouse is "lost" without the other. If a woman has a deep, unmet need to feel important, then having her husband incapable of functioning without her gives the illusion of meeting that need.

However, when a wife dares to give her man space and grace, it unleashes a freedom that will take her breath away. If this is your situation, you will gain a new respect for your man because you no longer view him as a helpless child. And the more you view him as a grownup, full of all the virility of a healthy male, your sexual response will naturally increase. And, you will soon find that your need to be valued will be filled on a fresh and healthy level. Your husband will begin treating you like his lover and confidante and less like his mother. The gnawing need, once pseudo-filled by creating dependency, will then be overflowing with marital fulfillment the way God intended.

In the process of breaking the mother-wife cycle, examine your man and find out exactly what areas he really does need you to complete him. For instance, Daniel has asked me to help him pick out his clothes for Sunday morning. Helping him in such a personal way breeds an intimacy between us that comes because I am meeting his *genuine* need. In recent years, I have erred on the opposite side of this issue and not done enough to complete my husband. I thought, *He's a grownup. He can do it himself.* I never followed him around trying to control his attempts at domestic chores. However, I also missed out on blessings because I didn't realize that I could be a powerful resource in his life by completing him where he *truly needed* my touch.

So many women have created false needs in their husbands and then became convinced that the men couldn't make it on any level without them. These women do everything for their husbands but brush their teeth and button their shirts. If you are a mother-wife, then discovering what your husband really needs from you and what you have made him need might be difficult. The key is to only do what he can't do for himself because he lacks knowledge or ability. Every person is different, so there isn't a rigid list of jobs he can handle. Some men are gourmet chefs. Others can't boil water without burning up the pan. If your husband is disabled, then your list will be different from that of a woman whose husband is not disabled.

You might say, "Well, we've been in this pattern for 25 years, and it works for us. It's our way in marriage." I think that's a wonderful answer as long as—

1. Deep inside you don't resent your husband for being so helpless.

2. You don't want him to help more because you believe he never will. You're content with the status quo.

3. His dependency on you doesn't make you view him as inept.

4. You don't use the setup to gain control over your man's every move.

If you have a tendency toward being a controller, hang in there. It takes time to successfully implement change. If you are ready to move from being your husband's mother to being his wife, then the following suggestions will help.

Lovingly request that your husband help you with specific tasks. Hug your husband and say something like, "Honey, it would be such a huge help to me if you would _____." Then give him a nice kiss. Many men will readily agree to a sweet-spirited request. If being a mother-wife has been a cycle of many years, then start out by choosing tasks that are small and not of life-and-death importance. That way, if he doesn't fulfill the request, it won't be a major ordeal. For instance, if he leaves his dirty underwear lying around, and you ask him to please put them in the hamper and he doesn't, then the world won't end if he wakes up one day and doesn't have underwear because he never put them in the hamper to be laundered. Yes, he will be aggravated. And when he is, just smile and say, "But you agreed to put them in the hamper, remember?" Then give him another kiss and go back to what you were doing. Don't say another word.

Don't do the task yourself—even if he leaves it undone for several days...or several years. This is another reason it's important to start out with small tasks. If you are in the mother-wife cycle, your husband is used to your stepping in behind him and picking up the slack. Therefore, he might gladly agree to do whatever you ask then fall right back into the cycle of behavior with no intentions of being ornery. He's just used to you taking charge because you've enabled him to be that way. If you then come through and do what you asked him to do, you reinforce the cycle. For instance, he might buy more underwear, rather than putting the dirty ones in the laundry. That's fine. Sweep the dirty ones into a pile in the corner of the bedroom. They're *his* underwear, and he's an *adult*. I guarantee that he managed his underwear just fine before meeting you. If he winds up with mounds of underwear because he keeps buying new ones, that's great! Everybody needs a lot of underwear. If your friends come over and see the pile, so what! They're *your husband's* underwear! If your husband wants your friends to see his used BVDs, then that's *his choice*. Let him be an adult! My husband and I have resolved this problem. He has a basket in our room where he puts his clothes. He doesn't leave underwear lying around by any means, but he does enjoy draping his clothes into the basket—whether they're clean or dirty. I figure they're his clothes. He can do what he wants with them. More than once he's come up without a clean shirt or pair of pants. Then he'll either wash a load himself or put his clothes in the laundry room. Nobody dies; the world doesn't end.

Don't nag your husband about what you've asked him to do. This is another trait of the mother-wife. Men hate to be nagged. All it does is aggravate the husbands and then they resent their nagging wives. It also impedes intimacy. When the couple finally has sex, the wife is aggravated at the husband for not doing "whatever" when she asked, and the husband is aggravated at the wife for nagging him. (By the way, I haven't met a woman who likes to be nagged either!)

When your husband finally gets around to doing the task, don't correct his efforts. Don't gripe. Don't comment—except to thank him profusely and praise his efforts. Throwing in a juicy kiss and a warm hug doesn't hurt either.

Everytime you think, "My husband is helpless," correct yourself. Remind yourself that he is a grown man. He is not helpless. Say, "He is my lover, my confidante, and my friend. I *will* respect him and treat him as an adult!"

Base your respect on his character qualities, not on his domestic abilities or shortcomings. For instance, some women find it hard to respect a man who leaves his underwear in a pile in a corner. Yet the same man might have sterling qualities of the heart such as "love, joy, peace, patience, kindness, goodness, faithfulness, gentleness and self-control" (Galatians 5:22,23). Base your respect for your husband on his good traits.

Continually think "space and grace!" Remember, Jesus Christ gives us ample doses of grace and plenty of space to make our mistakes. When we make the mistakes and turn to Him for help, He gives us more grace to overcome our errors! *Be Christ to your husband!*

As your husband successfully moves from thinking of you as his mother-wife, he will gradually do more and more. Let him! When he says, "Honey, I'm going to give you the night off and barbecue." Say, "Great!" Then plop into a recliner and take the night off. Don't live out the "usual" barbecue story presented at the beginning of this chapter. I can guarantee the tomatoes won't be sliced like you'd slice them and the iced tea might be sweeter than you fix it, but let your husband be an adult and do things the way *he* wants to do them. Then praise him like crazy when he does! And remember, improvement comes with practice.

Remind yourself of what your husband does do. Even though my husband does quite a bit, there are still nights when I'm exhausted and standing in front of a sink full of dishes while he watches television. On those nights, I remind myself of the things my husband has done for me. Because he does accept responsibility around the house, this dissolves the temptation to be resentful. If you are just beginning to break the mother-wife cycle, and he has even begun doing one task for himself, then remind yourself of that new achievement.

Remember this cycle might take a year or two to break. Don't expect to break a cycle decades long in just one week! This will take time—especially if he and/or you watched your mothers be mother-wives. Remember...*space and grace!*

Decide right now not to utter another word of complaint to your husband—even if breaking the cycle seems impossible. If you continually emit an air of complaint, it will taint your marriage, ruin the atmosphere of your home, and destroy any chances for romance or an excellent sex life.

Don't define "breaking the cycle" as "my husband does what I want him to do." Breaking the cycle means that you stop being the mother and give your husband the freedom to make his own choices. That means that if he wants to leave his underwear in the corner of the room for two years then you let him. Your bedroom is his just as much as it is yours.

If you are a mother-wife, expect a shift in your relationship with your mother-in-law when you break the cycle. This could be a positive or negative shift. If you and your mother-in-law have had a silent battle over who gets to be your husband's mother, then your becoming a lover-wife will give your mother-in-law the freedom to be your husband's mother. The war will be over!

However, if your mother-in-law thinks that the only good wives are mother-wives, she might resent your becoming a lover-wife. *Usually,* though, if you'll allow her to be your husband's mother and give her the respect of consulting her on some issues, you'll find out that she just might purr like a kitten.

Right now, I am sitting at the computer. My husband put the kids to bed so I could work. Did he put them to bed at exactly the time I would have chosen? No. Did he get them to brush their teeth the way I would have? No. Is my little girl sleeping in her overalls, instead of her nightgown? Most likely.

If I were a mother-wife, I would have sat down at the computer and kept my ear tuned for all that was supposedly "going wrong" while my husband got the kids to bed. Then, when I heard the "inevitable upheaval," I would have gotten up from my writing and with an air of importance, I'd say, "If anything is done right around here, it looks like I've got to do it!" Then I would march

from my office, griping the whole time I was correcting everything my husband did "wrong." The kids would rebrush their
teeth *my* way (but not necessarily a *better* way). And my little girl
would be sleeping in a nightgown, rather than overalls. I would
also be behind on my deadline and resent my husband for not
supporting me in my writing. I would be thinking something like,
I take care of the kids and house all day long so he can work. Why
can't he show me equal respect and do the same for me? I'm not
asking that much. Just some respect. I didn't sign on to be his slave!

And my husband? If I were a mother-wife, by this point he
would have done what many men do. He would have gone to bed
and been blissfully sleeping by the time I got through "doing
everything right." Then I would go into our bedroom, stand with
my hands on my hips, glare at his sleeping form, and think something like, *When I married him all I did was take on a child!*

And that is called enabling the husband-child syndrome.

But I'm not a mother-wife, so that's not what I did tonight. I let
my husband take care of *his* children the way *he* saw fit. The world
did not end because he let them sit up late and watch TV with
him. Our dentist did not beat down the door because my husband didn't brush the children's teeth *my* way. And my little girl
will not be sent to a psychiatric ward because she sleeps in her
overalls. This is what space and grace is all about.

As a result, my husband treats me like his lover, not like his
mother. In the middle of getting the kids ready for bed, he took a
break and came to my office. He had a race-car toothbrush in one
hand when he asked, "Have you checked your e-mail?" I said, "No,
but I can!"

I suspected he must have sent me an electronic greeting card,
and I was delightfully right. The card featured a couple walking
along the beach at sundown. The caption read: "The ecstasy of
our love is in the moments we share." The tune playing was "I Just
Called to Say I Love You." And Daniel wrote:

!!!!!!!!WOW!!!!!!!!
Hey, Beautiful, just wanted to say how much fun I had today. You are the greatest!! What an enjoyable experience!!! I hope you enjoyed your nap; I sure did miss you while you were getting your beauty rest. Better watch out getting too much because I can't take you being much prettier. I need to be able to watch the road when we go to Indiana. I love you!!!
DWS

And that is the result of being a lover-wife!

A lover-wife...

- Allows her husband to be a man.

- Doesn't criticize or demean him.

- Treats him as her equal.

- Doesn't expect her husband to be a domestic genius but appreciates what he does.

- Bases her respect on her man's character, not on his performance.

- Doesn't nag.

- Views herself as her husband's equal.

- Sees the home as belonging equally to her husband and herself. She respects her man as an equal owner and allows him to be himself and have control of his stuff in his own home.

- Does everything in her power to enable her man in all areas.

- Lovingly voices her respect for domestic help, then gives her husband the space and grace to do it the way he wants.

- Never complains about what he has done.

- Expresses appreciation for every task her husband performs on her behalf.

- Reminds herself of all he does for her.

- Allows her mother-in-law to be her husband's mother.

- Allows her husband to be his mother's son. (Your husband needs to show loyalty and respect for his mother by supporting her and helping her, especially if his father is not alive.) A lover-wife doesn't compete or feel threatened when he spends time with his mother.

> *Strong, gentle, caring, loving you.*
> *You are my knight in shining armor,*
> *Though sometimes the shine is hard to see*
> *When daily hassles cloud the view.*
> *But you're always there—*
> *Steady, quiet, and sure.*
> *What would I do without you—*
> *My anchor, my playmate, my lover.*
> *How empty my life would be*
> *Without strong, gentle, caring, loving you!*

Reality Checks

Personal

I have a deep, dark confession. I do pick up my husband's dirty socks. In any marriage there are going to be a few personal idiosyncrasies that result in each spouse serving the other in a mundane task. My husband is forced to repeatedly close my closet door and turn off the light because my brain is apparently not programmed to perform these simple tasks. This is where the spirit of servanthood and unconditional love breeds health in a marriage. Yes, there are times when I deliver a glass of tea to my husband even though he is perfectly capable of doing that for himself; but, he also does the same for me. I am not a mother-wife so I'm free to choose to serve Daniel in love and respect. My husband, likewise, has the freedom to choose to serve me.

Concept

The principle of this chapter is not suggesting that a husband and wife shouldn't serve each other. What's crucial in a marriage is a healthy attitude toward service. There is a balance to be achieved. If the wife is doing all the serving, she becomes the mother-wife. A mother-wife cycle is not about Christlike love; it's about control. Ironically, a mother-wife usually resists a husband trying to serve her because that makes him less dependent upon her. But if a man and woman are both living the spirit of mutual submission and service, both spouses are free to be adults and help each other. This spirit of unconditional love doesn't keep score to make sure each person does exactly the same number of tasks for each other. Winston Churchill said, "The English never draw a line without blurring it." This also applies to couples who learn to compromise. "When a husband and wife come to believe that equality means splitting things precisely down the middle, then marriage becomes a contest of who can get a better deal."[2]

Spiritual

You might believe that becoming your husband's mother is a sign that you are fulfilling Paul's message about wives submitting to their husbands. In reality, the opposite is true. When a wife embraces a mother-wife mentality, she actually undermines her husband. She thinks of him as a helpless child rather than a grown man. In that mindset, her complete submission to him will be affected. She might be able to submit to a certain degree by outwardly supporting his decisions and trying to meet his sexual needs, but not to the degree the Lord requires from *both* partners for a healthy marriage. It's difficult to revere your husband if you think of him as helpless. (See chapter 4 for a complete discussion of true, biblical submission.)

Prayer Points for Romance

If you are a mother-wife...

♭ Pray that the Lord will give you the strength to release your husband to Him.

♭ Pray that God will replace any fear of release with the assurance of His presence.

♭ Pray for your husband that he will understand the transition from mother-wife to lover-wife and appreciate your efforts to make your marriage more healthy.

♭ Pray that you will have the patience to allow some things to go undone.

♭ Pray that you will have the power to give your husband space and grace.

Romantic Notions

When it snows, she has no fear for her household;
for all of them are clothed in scarlet.
PROVERBS 31:21

What I Did

I cleaned out Daniel's closet, donated most of his clothes to Goodwill—with his permission—then bought him a new wardrobe. Early in our marriage, I tried to buy clothes for my husband, but I had no clue about his taste. He often never wore what I bought because it didn't suit him or fit him right. I finally stopped trying. After nearly two decades of living with him, I finally have a clue about what he likes. I bought some basics in the gentlemen's section of a nice department store. For the upscale coats, ties, some shirts, and socks, I went to a distinguished men's store and told them about our activities and exactly the look my husband needed. The kind salesperson was a great guide in helping me choose quality clothing that would suit Daniel's taste and be in fashion.

My Reason

His wardrobe desperately needed an overhaul. Daniel has sacrificed so much for me—supporting me through obtaining a master's degree and believing in me while I slaved away for eight years to make a profit from writing. After eight years of rejections, my writing career exploded, so I wanted to spend a significant amount of my money on him as a microscopic means of showing my appreciation for his steadfast support of me and my dreams. For so many years, we had sacrificed and worn what we could find on the sales rack and at garage sales. I really wanted him to feel pampered.

How I Felt

The whole time I was making the purchase, I felt like the Lord was right there with me. If ever a shopping trip was God-ordained, it was that one. I sensed such a steady assurance that I was doing exactly what I was supposed to do. I must say that I enjoyed shopping for Daniel more than I ever enjoyed shopping for myself.

The Obstacles I Overcame

I had my four-year-old with me during most of the shopping experience. She was tired and hung on me and whined and cried and generally expressed her disapproval of having to exercise self-control in, of all places, men's shops! What a boring place for a four-year-old. But I stuck to my plan and continued my quest in placing my husband's needs as a top priority. Thankfully, the salespeople were understanding. And well they should be—I left behind some significant funds!

My Husband's Response

The main shopping event was when I brought home the haul. My husband came home that day hesitantly expecting to see the results of my efforts. He knew I had planned to go to the men's shop, but life can be unpredictable when small children are around. When he asked about the shopping, I beamed and led him to our bed, which was covered by his new clothes. He was absolutely thrilled!

What I Wish I Had Done

I wish I had understood his need for me to complete him on this level a long, long time ago. For this particular man, my shopping for him and coming home with a complete wardrobe for him spoke my adoration for him on a very deep level. I used to think, *Well, he's a grownup. He can dress himself.* Even though that's true, this was a special area I could help him in. Something really fun takes place when a man needs his wife's help with his wardrobe, and she graciously agrees to meet that need. By the way, when my husband chooses to dress himself, I *never* change his choices unless he asks for advice!

Budget Suggestions

This one was expensive. Many couples with small children, whether employed outside the home or in, simply don't have a lot of extra money. Five years ago, if I had read this section, I would have thought, *Get in the real world, woman!* If you can't afford a major wardrobe overhaul, think about saving some money to buy your husband a special suit, item of clothing, or anything you know he would love. If you aren't employed, stash away $10 here or there for several months until you have squeezed together enough to make a special purchase. The sacrifice is well worth the glimmer of awe in your husband's eyes. And make this a "just because" gift—not a Christmas or birthday present.

Special Note

I have a pastor friend who recently told me that he dresses his wife. He does exactly what I did for Daniel. My friend goes to a nice women's shop and has a particular woman he consults with. She sells him the things his wife needs for ministry and travel. He enjoys buying new clothes for his wife, and she appreciates his completing her on this level. This is a good example of how marriage is really about looking for healthy ways to meet each other's needs, whatever they might be.

4
Love's Secret

Submit to one another out of reverence for Christ.
EPHESIANS 5:21

Don't Touch That Page!

FRANKLY, IF I WERE READING THIS BOOK instead of writing it, I would look at the key verse and roll my eyes. *Here we go again! Another person harping on submission!* I have heard enough unbalanced views on this subject to last a lifetime. So before we go any further, let me assure you that the one-sided, subservient messages you have probably been taught are not what you will read in this chapter.

I have read and heard numerous people blame just about every problem in a marriage and household on the wife and her lack of submission. Furthermore, I've been heartsick when I hear women come away from conferences completely convinced that they are the primary problem in their marriage. On the surface, a lopsided view of submission might sound scriptural. It might look scriptural. After all the New Testament *does* tell wives to submit to their husbands. But on a deeper level, this one-sided view of submission will sap the life out of any marriage and leave no room for healthy sexuality or even a hint of honest romance.

Problems arise on this slippery subject when the key verses on submission are pulled out of context and not viewed in light of all the Scriptures on marriage and relationships. Too often this method has been used to justify demeaning, dominating, and deprecating women. This also completely ignores several key Bible verses...

> Also a dispute arose among them as to which of them was considered to be greatest. Jesus said to them, "The kings of the Gentiles lord it over them; and those who exercise authority over them call themselves Benefactors. But you are not to be like that. Instead, the greatest among you should be like the youngest, and the one who rules like the one who serves. For who is greater, the one who is at the table or the one who serves? Is it not the one who is at the table? But I am among you as one who serves" (Luke 22:24-27).

> For by the grace given me I say to every one of you: Do not think of yourself more highly than you ought, but rather think of yourself with sober judgment, in accordance with the measure of faith God has given you. Just as each of us has one body with many members, and these members do not all have the same function, so in Christ we who are many form one body, and each member belongs to all the others (Romans 12:3-5).

> Do nothing out of selfish ambition or vain conceit, but in humility consider others better than yourselves. Each of you should look not only to your own interests, but also to the interests of others. Your attitude should be the same as that of Christ Jesus: Who, being in very nature God, did not consider equality with God something to be grasped, but made himself nothing, taking the very nature of a servant, being made in human likeness. And being found in appearance as a

man, he humbled himself and became obedient to death—even death on a cross! (Philippians 2:3-8).

Husbands, love your wives, just as Christ loved the church and gave himself up for her....In this same way, husbands ought to love their wives as their own bodies. He who loves his wife loves himself (Ephesians 5:25,28).

Submit to one another out of reverence for Christ (Ephesians 5:21).

So in everything, do to others what you would have them do to you, for this sums up the Law and the Prophets (Matthew 7:12).

Love is patient, love is kind. It does not envy, it does not boast, it is not proud. It is not rude, it is not self-seeking, it is not easily angered, it keeps no record of wrongs. Love does not delight in evil but rejoices with the truth. It always protects, always trusts, always hopes, always perseveres. Love never fails (1 Corinthians 13:4-8).

In light of these verses, there are no biblical grounds to hold one sex more accountable than the other when it comes to submission. According to H. Norman Wright, "A loving husband is willing to give all that is required to fulfill the life of his wife. His love is ready to make any sacrifice for her good. The man's first responsibility is to his wife. His love for her enables him to give himself to her."[1] Webster's dictionary defines submission this way: "To offer oneself of *one's free will;* to defer to another's wishes, opinions." James wrote, "So faith without deeds is dead" (James 2:26). Love without submission is also dead.

Submission is a two-way street. According to Dr. Stan Toler, "The time has come for a balanced view on submission. No marriage will remain healthy without heavy doses of submission from *both* husband and wife."[2] According to The Quest Study Bible, "A submissive spirit runs counter to society's values and it always has. However, it remains God's standard for all believers—male and female—for all time."[3] The Bible stresses this truth by telling believers, including husbands and wives, to submit to the needs of each other. According to Lawrence Richards, "All too often the debate in modern times has focused on the wrong questions. How much authority does the husband possess? How is the wife to submit? Can a wife work if her husband disapproves? Does the man have the right to discipline (or beat) his wife?...Paul is arguing that, within the church, each person, whatever his role in society, owes a debt of mutual submission to others. This debt can only be paid by infusing every relationship with *mutual commitment*. The wife owes duties to her husband, but the husband owes his wife a love which puts her needs on a par with his own, and puts her growth and development ahead of his own."[4]

When asked about marriage, Jesus Christ underscored the truths of these principles by pointing to God's original intent for marriage: "Moses permitted you to divorce your wives because your hearts were hard. But it was not this way from the beginning" (Matthew 19:8). In the beginning, God said, "For this reason a man will leave his father and mother and be united to his wife, and they will become one flesh" (Genesis 2:24). After the fall, God spoke of the *consequences* of sin when He told the woman, "[Your husband] will rule over you" (Genesis 3:16). However, Jesus came to deliver us from the carnal mind. He came to spiritually set us free from the curse of Adam and Eve. And when asked about marriage, Jesus Christ pointed to the way God originally intended a husband and wife to be. Any Christian man who believes part of his job is to control or rule his wife compromises the very essence of Christ's unconditional *(agape)* love. A man who loves his wife so much that he would die for her will *never* condescend her.

Throughout Scripture, we see Jesus concentrating on washing feet, serving others, and restoring relationships. He is the role model for husbands and wives.

In the Genesis 2:18 account of God's decision to create Adam a helper, the word "helper" would be better translated "a power like it, facing it," says Bible scholar Joseph Coleson.[5] The Reflecting God Study Bible underscores this interpretation: "The word 'helper' does not imply subordination; indeed, it is often used of God himself (Psalm 33:20; 70:5; 121:2)."[6] God created men and women to be equals with equal value and to cleave to one another as husband and wife, each setting aside his or her own needs in deference for the other (Genesis 2:24). St. Augustine said, "If God meant woman to rule over man, He would have taken her out of Adam's head. Had He designed her to be his slave, He would have taken her out of his feet. But God took woman out of man's side, for He made her to be a helpmate and an equal to him."[7] This is the reason Paul wrote, "Husbands, love your wives, just as Christ loved the church and gave himself up for her."

Unequal submission in a marriage cannot coexist with the basic truths of a gospel that repeatedly admonishes men and women to die to sin, be crucified with Christ, allow God to transform their minds, and place others above themselves. Paul writes, "I have been crucified with Christ and I no longer live, but Christ lives in me. The life I live in the body, I live by faith in the Son of God, who loved me and gave himself for me" (Galatians 2:20).

Both men and women are created in the image of God.
When we scorn one another because
of gender, we scorn someone who was
created in the image of God.
That means we ultimately scorn God Himself.

Despite contradictory evidence, many people still use the Bible to "prove" their gender prejudices. It is far too common to hear presentations where only selected Scriptures were chosen to support domineering attitudes. I have come away from such sessions feeling degraded and a lesser being in God's eyes. As distraught as I have been in those situations and as much as I believe that overbearing attitudes fly in the face of Scripture, I must acknowledge that women have also been guilty of extremism.

Female chauvinism, male chauvinism, racial/cultural prejudices, and economic snobbery are all branches off the same tree—a tree called selfishness. This selfishness will spread its poisonous roots through the soil of a marriage and destroy its foundation. As deeply concerned as I am over some men trying to validate their male chauvinism through twisting the Word of God and ignoring numerous key passages, I am as deeply disturbed over women who adopt a "down with men" view in an attempt to be superior to men or to overcompensate for male chauvinism. The fact that submission has sometimes been taught without balance does not nullify the Word of God. Wives are still told to submit to their husbands. Furthermore, the misrepresentation of submission does not justify returning a man's chauvinistic attitude with a female version of the same. I have witnessed chauvinism surfacing among Christian women in a variety of ways, including:

- Rolling the eyes and saying, "That's just like a man"

- Telling jokes that put men down

- Dishonoring husbands by scorning their needs

- Treating husbands as if they were children

- Trying to control husbands

- Believing women really are superior to men

- Joining in a "let's complain about men" gab session

- Not respecting and reverencing husbands

- Discrediting husbands' decisions, dreams, and masculinity

- Criticizing husbands in front of children and friends

- Not speaking constructive criticism to a husband in private and in love

- And, from little girls, "Girls rule, boys drool."

And now comes the moment of brutal honesty. I have been guilty of some of these. However, God in His mercy and love did to me what He reserves for only the most strong-willed of His children. He figuratively took me to a football stadium, drop-kicked me through the goalposts, and said over the loud speaker, "Now that I have your attention—stop the female chauvinism." *I stopped!*

Chauvinism is the antithesis of submission and God's love. It cannot coexist with unconditional love. As already stated in chapter 1, unconditional love and acceptance is the first love need for both a husband and wife.[8] As Christian spouses, the Lord calls us to higher ground, a place where He is Lord and we honor, value, and respect each other as equal heirs in the kingdom of God: "There is neither Jew nor Greek, slave nor free, male nor female, for you are all one in Christ Jesus" (Galatians 3:28).

Now, take a moment to appreciate the ways your mate expresses his submission to you. Here's my list…

- For years, my husband supported me while I finished graduate school. He continued the support as I worked to establish a successful at-home writing career.

- He drops everything at work and comes to my rescue when I have a flat tire.

- He graciously gives me his spoon at the Dairy Queen so I can eat part of his blizzard—because I really didn't want a whole treat, just a few bites of *his*.

- He occasionally offers to iron my skirt on Sunday morning.

- He doesn't push sexual issues if I am not feeling well.

- He doesn't complain if I am under a deadline and decide to "cook" sandwiches for dinner. And, even better, he occasionally takes charge of dinner and cooks or orders a pizza.

What Does Submission Have to Do with Romance?

> Wives, in the same way be submissive to your husbands so that, if any of them do not believe the word, they may be won over without words by the behavior of their wives, when they see the purity and reverence of your lives. Your beauty…should be that of your inner self, the unfading beauty of a gentle and quiet spirit, which is of great worth in God's sight (1 Peter 3:1-4).

According to this verse, submission is influence, submission is beauty, submission is of great worth to God. It is also the key to your husband's heart and the avenue through which romance will flourish. And if your husband is not a Christian, be an example to him, intercede through prayer for him, and never nag him about his lack of spiritual interest. (Men hate to be nagged. So do women!) God knows that if a wife is to influence her husband, then *submission,* not nagging, is the key. It's also the key to heightened romance and excellent sex.

According to Linda Dillow in her book *Creative Counterpart,* "Submission is many times the key to sexual response....[Furthermore] sexual response at the physical level is the equivalent of submission at the psychological level."[9] This worked beautifully for me when I stopped worrying about whether or not my husband was really loving me as Christ loved the church and I quit focusing on whether or not Daniel was meeting my needs. Instead, I followed the leading of the Holy Spirit and submitted— not only physically, but also emotionally and mentally. I turned my heart toward meeting my husband's needs. At that point, our sex life exploded. One night my husband said, "I don't know what you have done, but you have done it!"

When it comes to sex, submission is electric. When it comes to romance, submission is magic. *Submission is unconditional love in action.* A wife who experiences this kind of love for her husband is eager to meet his needs. Most men who see their wives striving to meet their needs and pouring energy into the romance of a marriage will respond by extending their hearts and enveloping their wives in love and submission to their needs. At this point, a marriage will sparkle with a God-ordained romance that outshines the glitter of jewels.

*When Boaz had finished eating and drinking and was in good
spirits, he went over to lie down at the far end of the grain pile.
Ruth approached quietly, uncovered his feet and lay down. In the
middle of the night something startled
the man, and he turned and discovered a woman
lying at his feet. "Who are you?" he asked.
"I am your servant Ruth," she said. "Spread the corner of your gar-
ment over me, since you are a kinsman-redeemer." "The LORD
bless you, my daughter," he replied. "This kindness is greater than
that which you showed earlier: You have not run after the younger*

men, whether rich or poor. And now, my daughter, don't be afraid.
I will do for you all you ask. All my fellow townsmen know that
you are a woman of noble character."

RUTH 3:7-11

The Specifics of Submission

The words "noble character" in Ruth 3:11 also appear in
Proverbs 31:10, "A wife of noble character who can find? She is
worth far more than rubies." "Noble character" is translated from
the Hebrew word *chayil,* and it holds nuances of meanings such
as might, strength, power; able, valiant, virtuous, valor; army, host,
forces; and riches, substance, and wealth. I stand a little taller when
I realize that chayil is used to refer to Ruth as well as the Proverbs
31 woman. Indeed, God created women with a strength and
power He intends them to use for His glory and the honor of their
husbands.

One of the most powerful acts we can accomplish in our marriages is submission. This is not an act of weakness—it is an act of
strength that will revolutionize a marriage. Submission offers husbands the security they need to completely release their hearts to
their wives. Few men love with abandon until they know their
wives are loyal. Submission speaks loyalty to a man. Loyalty and
respect. Respect and honor. Notice Boaz's reaction to Ruth, "And
now, my daughter, don't be afraid. I will do for you all you ask."
When they see submission in action, many Christian men will
want to serve their wives.

Once you experience the heightened romance it releases into
your relationship, you'll be looking for ways to demonstrate submission. Here are some suggestions for healthy submission and
the characteristics of unhealthy submission.

Healthy Physical Submission

    ♭ Wear your hair in a style that pleases your husband.

- Wear your makeup to please your husband. Ask him if there's something he would like you to change or add.

- If your mate makes positive comments on a dress style, wear that style as often as possible.

- Choose lingerie and perfume you know he enjoys.

- Within reason and to the best of your ability, try to keep your body the size he prefers.

Unhealthy Physical Submission

- Your husband dictates to you how you will dress, wear your hair, what perfume you will wear, and whether or not you will wear makeup and how much you will wear.

- He's never happy with your body.

- He physically abuses you. In turn, you cower and "submit," but deep inside, you resent him. (This is not biblical submission. This is being intimidated and abused. Healthy submission cannot be forced. It is an act of the will and is freely given without resentment. That's why healthy submission is so appealing and beautiful.)

Healthy Emotional Submission

- Readily and freely express your love to your husband. My goal is to tell my husband that I love him every day.

- Tell him he's the only man for you. I often tell my husband that if I met him for the first time, I would flirt shamelessly until he asked me out on a date.

- Share your disappointments and triumphs, your laughter and tears.

Unhealthy Emotional Submission

꙳ You put on a happy face and pretend everything is fine in your relationship when it isn't. (This is not healthy submission; it is living a lie.)

꙳ You are afraid to tell your husband how you really feel because you equate submission with going along with everything he says. (Please realize that you can maintain a godly, submissive spirit even when detailing negative emotions. Hiding emotions is not healthy submission; it is a manifestation of fear and only makes a problem worse.)

꙳ If your husband emotionally abuses you, you never confront him or ask him to stop.

Healthy Mental Submission

꙳ When you think of your husband, center your thoughts on how you can make his life better.

꙳ When tempted to look at other men, don't take the second look. Be loyal to your husband.

꙳ When you see your husband's faults, choose to focus on his positive traits. If the faults must be addressed, do so lovingly and with respect.

꙳ Make a mental note to daily praise your husband. (I repeatedly tell my husband he's a great man and an excellent father.)

Unhealthy Mental Submission

꙳ Your husband has convinced you that if you have any thoughts of your own you are not a godly wife.

- ꝑ You are condemned for wanting any kind of fulfillment—except in relation to him.

- ꝑ He has so intimidated you that you are afraid he can read your mind. (This is not healthy submission; this is mind control and mental torment.)

Healthy Romantic Submission

- ꝑ Read chapter 1 again and put it into practice.

- ꝑ View yourself as your husband's own personal flirt.

- ꝑ Extend as much energy into the romance of your marriage as you would your favorite hobby. Or make romancing your husband your favorite hobby.

Unhealthy Romantic Submission

- ꝑ Your husband belittles most of what you do, including your attempts at romance, so you work yourself overtime trying to please him. Nothing ever does. (This is not healthy submission; this is a cycle of codependency and perfectionism.)

Healthy Sexual Submission

- ꝑ You try to meet your husband's sexual needs.

- ꝑ You learn what he enjoys in bed and repeat it often.

- ꝑ You don't always wait for him to be the initiator. (When I asked my husband if he likes it when I come on to him, he just looked like he had won a million bucks and said, "Oh, yeah!")

- ꝑ You don't entertain sexual fantasies about other men.

Unhealthy Sexual Submission

- ᚷ Your husband forces you to have sex with him.

- ᚷ You are repeatedly asked to perform sexually for your husband's pleasure, and he is oblivious to your enjoyment or your emotional needs.

- ᚷ Your husband includes violence as a part of sexuality.

- ᚷ He is involved in pornography and expects you to participate.

- ᚷ Your husband pressures you to perform sexually in ways you're not comfortable with.

Healthy Spiritual Submission

- ᚷ Spiritually, we are to *submit to the Lord first.* We are to turn to Him, not our husbands, for salvation. (See chapter 2.)

- ᚷ We are called to submit to our husbands as to Christ. This means that we encourage and honor our husbands and respect their decisions.

- ᚷ Pray for your husband daily.

- ᚷ Make major decisions together. If you feel the Lord speaking specifically to you about a given decision, share that with your husband. Reasonable Christian men will listen to the wisdom of a godly wife.

Unhealthy Spiritual Submission

- ᚷ Your husband expects you to submit even if his decision is morally questionable.

- You have been told that if your husband asks you to go against the Word of God you should. (This is not biblical submission; it is disobedience to the Word of God.)

- You've been taught that if you sin because you are submitting to your husband's wishes, God will hold your husband accountable, not you. (This is not true. See the story of Ananias and Sapphira [Acts 5:1-10]. God holds the husband and wife equally responsible for their sin.)

- You have put your husband in the place of God and expect him to be as perfect as God.

If any of these examples of unhealthy submission typifies your marriage, begin by praying for yourself, your marriage, and your spouse. Second, speak the truth in love. Tell your husband that his treatment of you is killing the romance in your marriage and perhaps even killing your love, if that applies. Seek solid, Christian, professional counseling. Implement only healthy submission if possible. Read Laurie Hall's book *The Cleavers Don't Live Here Anymore* (Servant Publications).

My lover is radiant and ruddy, outstanding among ten thousand. His head is purest gold; his hair is wavy and black as a raven. His eyes are like doves by the water streams, washed in milk, mounted like jewels. His cheeks are like beds of spice yielding perfume. His lips are like lilies dripping with myrrh. His arms are rods of gold set with chrysolite. His body is like polished ivory decorated with sapphires. His legs are pillars of marble set on bases of pure gold. His appearance is like Lebanon, choice as its cedars. His mouth is sweetness itself; he is altogether lovely. This is my lover, this my friend.

SONG OF SONGS 5:10-16

Reality Checks

Personal

I would love to tell you that I have always completely understood and practiced wifely submission. But, honestly, I have spent more time exasperated over its being taught without balance than actually experiencing it. When I heard someone drone on in order to prove a dominating stance, I immediately dismissed the discussion and the concept. At last, the Holy Spirit gently showed me that my disagreement with the misinterpretations of submission didn't mean I was exempt from practicing what the Bible teaches. Only in recent years have I embraced this powerful truth and unleashed a new level of love between my husband and me. *Submission is unconditional love in action,* lived out by a wife and a husband.

Spiritual

The level of submission discussed in this book cannot and will not be achieved without a radical attitude change and obedience to God. If a woman will not submit to the one who created her, she will not submit to her husband. Likewise, if a man will not submit to the Lord, he will never be able to love his wife with the sacrificial, submissive love Jesus Christ exemplified on the cross. Only through abandonment to the Lord and an intimate walk with Him do we gain the power to submit to our spouses.

Real Life

You might say, "But my husband is doing nothing to fulfill my needs. He is not loving me the way Christ loved the church. He's just plain selfish. And as far as he's concerned, Ephesians 5:21— "submit to one another"—does not exist! And romance? Are you kidding! He couldn't care less!"

I acknowledge you are in a tough situation. Consider for a moment that the Bible sets up equations for relationships. For instance, the equation for a relationship and reconciliation with

God is: Jesus Christ died for our sins + our repentance and receiving His forgiveness = eternal life, joy, and a personal relationship with Him. Jesus Christ died on the cross for us knowing full well that some people would still reject Him. Yet He did it anyway; He *chose* to do His part. But in order for us to receive a relationship with Him, we have to obey His wooing and *choose* to do our part of the equation. We have to repent and ask His forgiveness. Our lack of doing our part does not change His part. He still died for us, He still extends forgiveness to us, He still wooes us to Himself.

The same holds true in your marriage relationship. Wives submit to husbands + husbands submit to wives = marital harmony, heightened sexuality, and great romance. You can submit to your husband, and he may not immediately respond with his part of the equation. However, that does not exempt you from performing the part of the equation God has called you to perform.

Rest assured, the Word of God is faithful and true. When 1 Peter 3:1-4 says our submission is a powerful influence, it means our *healthy* submission is a powerful influence. Dare to put biblical submission into practice. Over time, you will be astounded by the results!

Prayer Points for Romance

If you are struggling with submission, the following will empower you to obey the Word of God.

- If you have embraced the female chauvinist mindset, pray that the Lord will cleanse your heart and mind of this erroneous attitude.

- If your husband has embraced the male chauvinistic mindset, pray that the Lord will convict him of his wrong attitude.

- Pray that the Lord will give you the strength to choose healthy submission to your husband, even if he is not fulfilling his part of the marriage equation.

- Pray that God will help you love your husband unconditionally.

- Ask the Lord to show you every day at least one way you can romantically demonstrate your devotion, love, and submission to your husband.

Romantic Notions

*We must grow in love and to do this
we must go on loving and loving and giving
and giving until it hurts—the way Jesus did.
Do ordinary things with extraordinary love.*[10]

MOTHER TERESA, 1999

Note: The reason the following act of submission was so powerful is because I had not made a habit of doing anything of this nature. While you read the suggestion, try to think of something you have never done or almost never done to show your submission to your husband. If this works, then great. But if your husband has insisted that you wait on him for years, then waiting on him more is not going to prove a thing.

What I Did

My husband was sitting on the couch, looking tired and a little down. I sat in his lap, ran my fingers through his hair, and asked him if there was anything I could get him. Tea? Water? Anything I could do to make his life better?

My Reason

This was my way of demonstrating my love and submission to Daniel. I have never been inclined to wait on other people, and this was a serious act of submission on my part.

How I Felt

Making myself available for his service left me feeling overwhelmed with love for him. This offer was submission in action and, therefore, an expression of unconditional love. I glowed with the joy flowing from his eyes.

The Obstacles I Overcame

There was a time when I would have resisted offering to wait on Daniel. I have seen husbands who use their wives as slaves or personal servants, and I always thought that was so unfair. (I still do.) Even though Daniel has never been that type of husband, my main obstacle was my fear of my submission being misused, taken for granted, or abused.

My Husband's Response

He virtually "glowed in the dark" and assured me he didn't need anything at the moment. But he *did* enjoy my visit on his lap. The next day, I received a romantic e-mail card from him that read:

> Debra,
> I wanted to tell you that I missed you today, and I wish that we could have spent some time alone together! You are the BEST and most wonderful LADY in the world, and I feel very thankful to be able to call you my wife! I hope that your day is filled with many blessings and many good moments. I will miss you while

you speak to your friends and fellow writers. I will be thinking of you and your wonderful touch and soft skin. Your book that I just finished reading was very good, and I am really impressed with the professional job that you did! You are really getting better and better at all that you do. Have a wonderful day and remember that I love you!!!

What I Wish I Had Done

I should have tossed aside my fears about submission and done this type of thing years before.

Budget Suggestions

This suggestion is one of the most costly of the whole book. It will cost you your whole heart…releasing everything you are to God…releasing your love to your husband…releasing your pride and fear to the Lord.

Communication and Sex

How is your beloved better than others,
most beautiful of women?
SONG OF SONGS 5:9

I NEVER INTENDED TO HARM ANYONE. Honest. I simply wanted to pamper myself a bit, so I squeezed a lavish amount of baby oil into my warm bath and lay back to enjoy the moment.

After my "moment" was over, I drained the oversized, fiberglass tub, dried off, and started getting ready for bed. My dear, unsuspecting husband, who is built like a football player, hopped into the tub and closed the shower curtain. Then the strangest thing began to happen. I say "began to happen" because the event was something that should have happened in a split second but, instead, it kept going and going and going. The first thing I heard was a hard thud. Then a bum-bum bounce conk-crash. Next, some undefined body part, more than likely a hand, elbow, or foot, slammed into the blue shower curtain. It puffed outward like a mushroom. More thudding. A flop. A few knocks. And another body part assaulted the shower curtain. A roll. A rumble. The sounds of shampoo bottles toppling into the tub. Then silence. Poor Daniel never uttered a sound during the whole ordeal.

Before the initial thud, I had been about to brush my teeth. Well, let's just say that little chore was postponed. I stood perched in front of the tub, not knowing whether to laugh, cry, or *run!* I have strong tendencies toward hilarity, so I was seriously contemplating laughter.

I heard dear Daniel attempting to stand. At this point, he still had not spoken one word. Then he dashed aside the shower curtain and glared at me. Daniel's eyes are pretty much a normal shade of green. However, they had taken on a strange monster glow much like a dragon's eyes in a nightmare. The only thing that distracted me from his glowing orbs was the round shiny spot about the size of two silver dollars on his reddened cheek. Baby oil, of course.

As the irate stare continued, I forced myself to keep my face impassive. I strongly detected that laughter at this point could be fatal. Finally, Daniel yanked the shower curtain back into place. Still trying to repress the hilarity, I bit my lips until they ached.

My husband turned on the shower. The warm water must have washed away his fury, for soon I heard a chuckle, a chortle, and then outright laughter. Realizing the coast was clear, I allowed my own amusement to spew forth.

Only when his shower was over and we were both weakened with laughter did I learn the "inside story."

"I just couldn't stop falling," he said. "Everything I grabbed was slick. I would think I was going to stop then I'd slide up one side of the tub and back to the other." He paused to snicker. "It was like I was a seal or something."

Thankfully, a crack in the bathtub was the only lasting injury. (Do I even need to mention that I have refrained from adding baby oil to my bath to this very day?)

Often our attempts to communicate within our marriages are like Daniel's uncontrolled flopping in the baby-oiled bathtub. According to H. Norman Wright in *Communication: Key to Your Marriage*, "Communication specialists point out that when you talk with another person there are actually six messages that can come through:

1. What you mean to say.

2. What you actually say.

3. What the other person hears.

4. What the other person thinks he or she hears.

5. What the other person says about what you said.

6. What you think the other person said about what you said."[1]

After reading this list I felt like my brain flopped in an oily bathtub. No wonder so many men and women claim their spouses don't understand them!

Regardless of the pitfalls in communication, one thing remains true: The healthier the communication between a couple, the deeper the intimacy and the more exciting the physical union. Communication encompasses not only what we say but also our every expression, gesture, and action.

Sadly, many couples are living in a world of their own with little or no healthy communication. The only message each spouse shares is, "I don't want to communicate."

According to Gary Rosberg, "Couples who are struggling with conflict, disappointment, lack of communication, isolation, and pain report that their sexual relationship really is a barometer of the problems in the marriage."[2] When a woman refuses to meet her husband's sexual needs, she is communicating, "I don't care. I don't need you. I don't love you." In turn, men then withdraw from their wives and focus on their own interests and needs— their careers, their hobbies, and perhaps even pornography or the beds of lovers. I am in no way saying that a man isn't responsible for his own sin before God. He is. However, a wise woman realizes that her husband's raging need for sex will leave him vulnerable to moral failure if she does not commit to fulfilling his need. The man who is unfulfilled steadily distances himself from his wife. The chasm between the couple grows to mammoth proportions as the isolation and loneliness intensifies. Conversely, *when a woman hurls energy into meeting her husband's sexual needs, she wows her man to the point that he will fall all over himself to meet her needs.*

Do you want meaningful conversation and communication with your husband? Then focus on selflessly meeting his needs. Give him really good sex. Don't just lie in bed and expect him to do all the work. The erroneous belief that women are recipients and not participants in the bedroom must be overturned if we are to really please our husbands. Christian couples should have the most exciting, most erotic sex life of anyone because *God created sex!* In "10 Things Your Man Really Wants in Bed," Pamela Lister states "enthusiasm" as secret number one.[3] That enthusiasm includes your willingness to drop everything for a spontaneous moment as well as initiating intimacy. Enthusiasm also encompasses expressing your excitement in bed. According to Lister, "When guys say they wish their wives would initiate more, they really mean they wish their wives were more aggressive, more obvious, more direct."[4]

"Wow" your man on a regular basis. Many times, women say, "If I did _____ my husband would be shocked!" You fill in the blank, then give him a "shock." An occasional shock does wonders for a man and escalates the quality of communication level in your marriage beyond the realms of anything you could imagine. Few men remain unchanged after a wife plots to "shock him" on a regular basis. I'm beginning to be able to spot a "shocked" man. He usually has this slightly goofy grin when his wife walks into the room, and the air between the two virtually crackles. And communication? Those two will be exhibiting positive communication vibes almost nonstop. Unfortunately, a "shocked" man is a rare find. (If you are floundering with what you could do to electrify your husband, chapter 9, "Exciting Encounters," offers a few creative ideas.)

Gary Rosberg suggests that "if a wife doesn't know what it takes to satisfy her husband, it is essential that she find out."[5] Many married couples don't discuss sex at all. Considering the huge part sex plays in a healthy marriage, not discussing the subject with your spouse will lead to a less-than-exciting, inhibited sex life. If you want to open the lines of communication, Rosberg lists seven questions that will stimulate conversation:

- "What would show you that I am interested in your sexual needs?"

- "How often do you need sexual intercourse?"

- "What satisfies you most about our sexual relationship?"

- "What do you need me to do more often?"

- "What do you need me to do less often?"

- "What does it mean to you if I initiate sex?"

- "If I am not ready for sex at the same time you are, how can I show that in a way that doesn't make you feel rejected?"[6]

Frankly, most of my deep, meaningful conversations with my husband happen after really great sex. Back in the good old days, they called it "pillow talk." There's no other time like the hour or so after physical union when I feel more close to my husband. The merging of our hearts, minds, and souls seems all the sweeter after the merging of our bodies. Most men who are brimming over with the aftermath of sexual fulfillment ooze with the desire to verbally share with their wives. Perhaps posing the previous seven questions during pillow talk would take advantage of an excellent opportunity for honest sharing. My husband and I also often share "pillow prayer" during this time. It never hurts to ask your husband to pray aloud that you will have wisdom in meeting his sexual needs. Before you know it, he'll be praying for himself in meeting your needs as well. The afterglow of a satisfying sexual union encourages golden communication on emotional, mental, and spiritual levels.

Don't distress, however, if this type of communication doesn't happen overnight. You might wow your husband for several months before he really starts sharing with you. But I would hazard a guess that most men aren't quite as hard-hearted as that. Remember, if you're only giving your husband sex to get something in return—even good communication—your motives will be tainted. I cannot overstress how important it is that you *selflessly* devote yourself to fulfilling your husband's needs and never abandon the quest for an excellent marriage.

Nurturing Oneness

We cultivate spiritual intimacy in our marriage through the traditional means—praying together, participating in a weekly Bible study with other couples, and enjoying Communion every Sunday. But more and more we are finding that the time we spend before falling asleep, when we snuggle close and share intimate conversation, is some of the most precious. Especially in our playful lovemaking, Christ's kingdom is brought into our hearts and into our marriage in a unique way. In lovemaking we become delightfully abandoned and vulnerably trusting. Excitement and

an overwhelming sense of oneness invade our lives as
we mutually nurture and frolic with curiosity and
awe—all very spiritual concepts as God teaches us
marvelous lessons about celebration and pleasure.
Meaningful touch often nurtures the deeper spiritual
parts of our being. Colossians 3:12-14 tells us to cultivate gentleness, kindness, humility, empathy, forgiveness, and, above all, love. In a marvelous manner, our
lovemaking helps us bring these qualities into our
marriage and has brought us closer to our Creator and
to the spiritual one-flesh partnership he desires. Thank
you, Lord![7]

Communication and Fidelity

Many experts divide communication into the realms of verbal
and nonverbal. Verbal communication includes what we say and
the noises we make. For instance, a cheerful laugh, scornful snort,
or an "oh brother" would be verbal communication, while rolling
the eyes, a soft touch, or a silent smile is nonverbal. Both forms of
communication carry a powerful message.

However, for the purposes of this book, allow me to divide
communication into two alternative groups: fidelity and infidelity.
Usually when we talk about issues of fidelity we immediately think
of sexual behavior. But fidelity spans a much wider sphere than
just what we do with our bodies. Our faithfulness to our mates
includes our thoughts, actions, attitudes, and words. Many
women would never dream of having an affair, even though they
may daily participate in verbal or nonverbal infidelity.

Think of every word you say as a bubble. Each bubble is full of
either slime or shine. If you live a life of verbal fidelity with your
mate, your words praise him, encourage him, and generally build
him up. If you live a life of verbal infidelity with your mate, then
your words will criticize, bite, and discourage him. After several

years of verbal infidelity, a man's heart will be so caked over with a thick layer of slime that he will eventually quit pouring energy into the marriage.

Communication fidelity goes much deeper than words. The Lord calls women of God to turn their hearts toward Him first, then pledge that their attitudes, thoughts, and actions also speak of an unshakable fidelity to their husbands. Few husbands will release their hearts to their wives unless they feel confident and safe in their unwavering loyalty. Where does your communication rank? Under fidelity or infidelity? Be honest with yourself as you read the characteristics of faithful communication, then pledge to regularly ask the Lord to empower you to a deeper level of loyalty to your man.

Also, while reading the following, please keep in mind that if you are experiencing sexual or physical abuse or a husband who is destroying you emotionally, I beseech you to call the police or close family members and leave in order to protect your own life or mental health and, if applicable, the lives of your children. The following sections are in no way encouragement for a woman in a seriously dysfunctional relationship to become codependent; rather, they are guidelines for turning an ordinary or waning marriage into something extraordinary. You may be thinking, *Well, women need this kind of fidelity as well.* To which, I shout a loud *yes!* In the preface, I suggested you ask your husband to read this book. This chapter is one of the reasons why. Please do not think I am presenting a one-sided admonishment on this subject. However, since I am writing to women, I am challenging *you* to do what is faithful and right regardless of what your husband does.

Faithful Verbal Communication

A woman of verbal fidelity lives by one rule: She speaks the truth in love. No matter what she says to her husband, it is couched in terms of love. If there is an issue in the marriage, she lovingly shares her concerns. She does not demean her husband for any reason. Any criticism is constructive and is bathed in prayer before being offered at all. Such a wife realizes that just because she sees an area where her husband can improve, she does not have license to immediately, swiftly, and concisely share it. She offers correction only if she honestly feels that the Lord is urging her toward it. Also, she recognizes that she isn't free of faults and that before she offers healthy comments to her mate, she must allow the Lord to carve her into His image. Remember, most men don't want a mother; they want a wife, lover, companion, and friend.

During any differences of opinion, a devoted wife avoids hurling insults or demeaning her husband's masculinity. A wife who honors verbal fidelity never degrades her husband's sexual performance. Instead, she lets him know with her words that she finds him attractive and satisfying. If there are troubled areas in the marriage that need to be discussed, the devout wife prays for an opportunity to share her hurts and needs with her husband then speaks up when the moment arises. A wife of such integrity will usually find that God opens doors for the issues to be discussed. Covering up true issues only creates an "infection" in the marriage that can eventually destroy the relationship. If and when a husband asks, "What's wrong, honey?" the verbally faithful lovingly shares her hurts and concerns.

In social situations, the woman who is verbally faithful to her husband never casually discusses him and his problems with her friends. She doesn't complain about him behind his back; she never cuts him down in public. A wife of such constancy never criticizes her husband in front of their children. If a problem in the marriage exists and she consults a professional, her words are humble, honest, and confidential. The woman who refuses to participate in verbal infidelity never allows the ties of her family of origin to supersede her bond with her mate. This includes not complaining to her mom and dad about her husband. Not only is that bad for the marriage, it also creates tension between the husband and his in-laws. Furthermore, a loyal wife doesn't talk with her girlfriends about her sex life unless there is a healthy reason for encouragement. A good example of healthy sharing on the subject lies in this very book. But the intimacies and joys of bedroom life should be left between her and her husband.

Faithful Nonverbal Communication

The wife who pledges nonverbal fidelity never uses her facial expressions as a means to control, insult, or belittle her mate. She refuses to play baby games such as the silent treatment as a means of "punishment." Such a woman gazes upon her mate with adoration and respect pouring from her eyes. She meets him at the end of the day with a smile and an appreciative hug. When he talks, she listens with an attentive heart and clear focus on his eyes. She uses her hands to stroke his face, give him a shoulder massage, or clasp his hand in hers. The woman who pledges nonverbal fidelity looks for ways to silently communicate that, next to God, her husband is the most important person in her life.

> *May the words of my mouth*
> *and the meditation of my heart be*
> *pleasing in your sight, O LORD,*
> *my Rock and my Redeemer.*
> PSALM 19:14

Rest assured that your man craves your undivided fidelity as much as you crave his. I've come to the conclusion that men have some kind of a verbal fidelity antenna that swiftly and immediately picks up when their wives aren't faithful in their words. A woman who pledges communication fidelity soon discovers that her husband becomes her best friend. She calls him first when something exciting happens. She doesn't make a habit of canceling plans with him to be with her other friends.

A husband with such a wife will never be forced to search for the loyalty and connection he craves from her from others. He will experience the human connection he craves from his wife. While connecting with friends of the same sex is important and healthy for both the husband and wife, the best and most intimate of friendships can and will happen within the marriage when a wife and husband pledge communication fidelity.

Do you wonder why being your husband's best friend is important? There are a variety of reasons—a fulfilling marriage, a life of joy, and a great love life. Another sobering reason comes from the fact that most affairs start with friendship.

> A full relationship requires a communication process in which both partners share and get to know all aspects of each other's lives. Getting to know another person intimately requires that one listen and come to appreciate all dimensions of the beloved. The relationship itself is strengthened through such an intimate sharing together. This includes learning to play together, to plan and dream together, to work toward future goals together. Spiritual oneness will come as the couple seeks God's presence and blessing in their… union.[8]

Socially, the woman who is wholly devoted to her mate doesn't grimace behind his back. She doesn't use gestures or expressions to belittle his character. In front of her children, she doesn't roll her eyes as he walks away. The faithful wife makes certain that when others are looking her every action speaks loyalty. Since actions speak louder than words, you usually can't fool people on this point; it's impossible to carry out a deception for very long. Fidelity is not about putting on a show. It stems from a heart pure before God and flows forth as a natural consequence of what's in the soul.

Reality Checks

Personal

I cannot end this chapter without being brutally honest. There was a time when I would discuss my man with my friends. Daniel said to me, "I felt like I was on trial." And I thought I was hiding my complaining! When I started living out fidelity of the mind and spirit, my husband became my best friend. It is intensely shameful for me to admit this, and I do it with tears of repentance and remorse in my eyes. I am being transparent because if you're caught in the trap of discontent, I want you to know you're hearing from a woman who has experienced it. I've tried being verbally unfaithful. It doesn't work. When you pledge fidelity of the heart, mind, and spirit, you will find your best friend is sharing your bed—and your bed will sizzle!

Communication

How much are you and your husband communicating? The following questions and your answers will reveal exactly how well you know your husband. If you know all of the answers or all but a couple, then you are most likely doing a fairly good job in communicating with your husband. If you find you are struggling, perhaps you should consider really getting to know your man. In *Angry Men and the Women Who Love Them*, Paul Hegstrom says that in his first marriage he and his wife were only acquaintances and nowhere close to an intimate relationship or even friendship. During their second courtship and marriage they became friends.[9] Are you and your husband best friends?

1. What is the happiest thing that has ever happened to your husband?

2. What has been the hardest experience of his life?

3. What are his secret ambitions, his goals for life?

4. What are his deep fears?

5. What about you does he appreciate most?

6. What traits of yours would he like to see changed?

7. What man or men does he most admire?

8. What are his spiritual struggles?

9. What does he like best in bed?

10. What's his favorite piece of your lingerie?

11. What's his favorite color? Favorite restaurant? Favorite dessert?

12. What's his favorite song?

13. What's his favorite sport?

14. Who is his favorite professional athlete?

15. What was his favorite class in high school and/or college?

16. When he was a child, what did he dream of doing?

17. What's his earliest childhood memory?

18. What's the one thing he would consider a sexual treat?

19. How does he feel about storms? Has he ever been in a tornado? Snowed in?

20. What brand of underwear does he prefer?[10]

If you aren't communicating on an intimate level with your husband, the time to begin is now.

Prayer Points for Romance

If you are struggling with issues of communication then the following prayer points will begin your journey to healthy interaction with your mate.

- Pray that the Lord will give you the fortitude to begin discussing sexual issues with your husband.

- Pray that God will empower you to abandon yourself to meeting your husband's sexual needs—even if he isn't meeting all your needs.

- Pray for the self-control to maintain communication fidelity.

- Pray that the Lord will show you ways to befriend your husband.

- Pray that any wounds from past communication infidelity will be healed in your marriage.

Romantic Notions

Do what you can, with what you have, where you are.
THEODORE ROOSEVELT

Here's an insightful idea from my friend Juanita Wells.

What I Did

I arranged for my husband and me to have a weekly day to relax together and share hobbies he enjoys. For us, that hobby was golfing and fishing.

My Reason

At the time, my husband was the pastor of his first church. He was physically ill with back spasms and costochrondritis, which are usually related to stress. It was apparent he needed to take a complete day off and relax. But it's hard to stay home and do that in a parsonage because the phone rings constantly, and his mind was focused on church relations. Pastors have to get away from the phone or not answer it, which he would not do if he were home. Also, I could see that if our relationship was to stay intact and we were to spend quality time together we needed to make it a priority to regularly take a complete day off together.

How I Felt

Refreshed! Our Monday golf or fishing excursion became our special haven from the pressures of the rest of the world.

The Obstacles I Overcame

The main obstacles were finances and working my occupation around his day off. I also had to get my husband to realize he should take a day off for his physical and mental health and that we needed "quality time" together. He was all for it if I could come up with the money, so I trimmed the budget to fit our need.

My Husband's Response

He thought I was generally wonderful. Also, after hours of interacting on the golf course or fishing, we usually experienced a really special time of physical intimacy.

What I Wish I Had Done

Even though we enjoyed our time alone, I look back and wonder if I should have found something that would have occasionally included our daughters.

Budget Suggestions

Depending on your hobby of choice, this could be free or cost thousands of dollars. I suggest you do whatever budget adjustments are necessary in order to afford this relationship builder. Once I cashed in a savings account I had sweated to build up in order to buy a fishing boat. That boat was worth at least a million dollars to our relationship. I now tell other women—especially pastors' wives—to note the hobbies their husbands enjoy most and learn to love them too.

The Controlling Factor

The thief comes only to steal and kill and destroy;
I have come that they may have life, and have it to the full.
JOHN 10:10

ACCORDING TO WILLIAM L. COLEMAN, female rhinos select their mates in a most unladylike manner. "She is nearsighted, so when she sees her beau she first backs up. Then she charges him at 30 miles an hour, hitting him broadside and knocking him to the ground. Then she proceeds to gouge and step on him. While he is literally bleeding and bruised he gets the message, 'She loves me!' The Christian woman is not this way. She is feminine. She is gentle, sweet, and kind because she knows what femininity is all about. There are very few men who would want a drill sergeant for a wife."[1] And, frankly, few wives enjoy husbands who adopt the female rhino's approach. I chat with wives all over the United States, and never once has one said, "I just love it when my husband steps on me and tries to control me." Just as much as women dislike being controlled, so many men also find grievance in living with domineering wives. This type of attitude is abuse whether manifested by the wife or husband.

Unfortunately, many marriages are nothing more than a battleground for power. Often Christian men and women stand at an altar before God and, between the two of them, promise to "love, honor, respect, and cherish." Then, three days to a year later, one mate is trying to dominate the other. What a disillusionment—especially when we know "cherish" means "treasure, esteem, appreciate, honor, prize, hold dear, value, revere, admire" and "respect" means "esteem, admire, affection, approval, homage, regard, honor, deference, adoration, revere." Amazing, isn't it, how close the meanings of these two words are.

Control is the antithesis of respecting or cherishing. A woman who tries to control her husband can in no way respect and revere him. According to Laura Doyle, "If you trust him—and respect his ideas rather than trying to control…I guarantee that you will be one step closer to fostering intimacy with your husband."[2] For a husband, this lack of a wife's control frees and empowers him to be all he can be in all his relationships, including marriage. Doyle further states, "Until you stop trying to run his life you'll never know what it's truly like to be married to your husband….If he feels disrespected, his natural instinct to provide, protect, and adore his wife is derailed. When a wife respects her husband, he naturally responds with more confidence in himself and gratitude for his wife. This makes him cherish her more and spend more time and effort memorizing the things that make her happy."[3] In *Each for the Other,* Bryan Chapell asserts, "The husband is not the only one who benefits from the respect a godly wife offers; she benefits too. The respect a wife offers her husband is the key to the deeper levels of marital bliss for which her own heart yearns…. Conversely the woman who does not offer her husband respect denies herself the potential for intimacy."[4] Chapell goes on to say, "Physical attraction, though powerful, will not maintain a relationship in which mutual respect has died."[5]

I believe that one of the signs that respect is dying or has never existed is when attempting to control the other person creeps in. "I want to control my spouse" is the same as saying, "I respect him so little that I will run over him." "I will use sex as a means to control" is the same as saying, "I have no regard for his needs or for God's design in creating my husband."

On the other hand, I often see Christian husbands exhibiting this attitude: "Genesis 3 says I get to rule over my wife, so I will control her. It's my God-given right." Meanwhile, some Christian wives are thinking, *I'm smarter than he is any day of the week. Nobody is going to control me! If anybody needs to be controlled, it's him! So, I'll use sex to control him. If he's a good boy and does what I want, I'll give him sex. If he doesn't do my wishes, then he won't get any.* And what God intended as a beautiful bonding between a man and woman turns into two people pulling against each other, trying to best each other, two people who never release their hearts to the other. When a husband respects his wife and a wife respects her husband they are fulfilling God's design for marriage.

> *Take away love and our earth is a tomb.*
> ROBERT BROWNING
>
> *Take away love and our marriages are a battleground.*
> DEBRA WHITE SMITH

The beauty of the New Testament, Holy Spirit-filled marriage is that rather than the Genesis 3 law of sin ruling, the Ephesians 5 law of submission, self-sacrifice, and unconditional love prevails. When Jesus Christ came into the world, He came to fulfill the Law of the Old Testament. And some parts of the Old Testament He fulfilled by proclaiming a new law—a law of love and grace. Paul clearly underscores this in Romans 13:8-10:

> Let no debt remain outstanding, except the continuing debt to love one another, for he who loves his fellowman [or spouse] has fulfilled the law. The commandments, "Do not commit adultery," "Do not murder," "Do not steal," "Do not covet," and whatever other commandment there may be, are summed up in this one rule: "Love your neighbor [and spouse] as

yourself." Love does no harm to its neighbor [or spouse]. *Therefore love is the fulfillment of the law* (emphasis added).

And Christ fulfilled this new law when He laid down His life for us: "God demonstrates his own love for us in this: While we were still sinners, Christ died for us" (Romans 5:8).

In Old Testament times, God's people were required to sacrifice animals as an offering for the atonement of their sins. When Christ died on the cross, He became the supreme sacrifice for all sins: therefore, the animal sacrifices of the Old Testament became unnecessary. As the law of Christ's sacrificial love revolutionized the atonement for sins, so the law of Christ's sacrificial love revolutionizes marriages.

The misuse of Genesis 3:16 as permission for a husband to dominate his spouse is unraveled by the New Testament truths found in verses such as Ephesians 5:21-33, where *both* spouses are called to lay down their rights for the other in submission, love, and sacrifice. In verse 31, Paul quotes God's Garden of Eden plan: "For this reason a man will leave his father and mother and be united to his wife, and the two will become one flesh." Jesus Christ said, "Moses permitted you to divorce your wives because your hearts were hard. But it was not this way from the beginning" (Matthew 19:8). According to Aida Spencer, "Although Christ may have changed our perspective toward the Old Testament's sacrificial laws he has by no means invalidated the authority and pertinence of the Old Testament. Almost all foundational questions find their answer in the early chapters of Genesis. Male–female relations are no exception."[6]

Whether male or female, the person who is trying to control another makes the other party miserable and puts him- or herself in bondage. It's a full-time job to control your husband. You have to continually keep tabs on him—his time, the money he spends, the people he talks to, his decisions, the car he drives, the music he listens to, the sports he enjoys, the hobbies he pursues....The list is never ending. A mate who tries to control the other is a prisoner of his or her own selfish desires —desires based on unrighteousness rather than the freedom Christ came to bestow upon all who believe.

First John 1:9 states, "If we confess our sins, he is faithful and just and will forgive us our sins and purify us from all unrighteousness." The purifying this verse refers to means to cleanse completely. While verses 8 and 10 say we are sinners and if we say we have not sinned we are lying, verse 9 clearly states that Jesus Christ died on the cross to purify and deliver us from sin. Therefore, verses 8 and 10 should never be used as an excuse to embrace a sinful mindset, which includes manipulation and controlling someone else. Every honest Christian will admit that there are times when he or she must ask for forgiveness from God and others. However, Jesus Christ came to enable both men and women to live above a *lifestyle* of sin to a life of dying to self, dying to the need to control, dying to the tendency to use sex as a weapon.

When Satan entered the Garden of Eden with an agenda to steal and kill, he also destroyed the marriage relationship. If a marriage is based on the idea that a husband has the right to be overbearing, then it's founded upon carnal rulership and control rather than love and sacrifice. We are actually basing our relationship on sin's bondage rather than on the freedom Christ bestows. The prophet Isaiah calls us to "seek the LORD while he may be found; call on him while he is near. Let the wicked forsake his way and the evil man his thoughts. Let him turn to the LORD, and he will have mercy on him, and to our God, for he will freely pardon. 'For my thoughts are not your thoughts, neither are your ways my ways,' declares the LORD" (55:6-8). God calls Christian men and women to a higher plane in their relationships—a plane where a wife and husband are pledged to adopt God's thoughts and ways and empower one another. In a healthy marriage no one holds all the power. Laurie Hall comments,

> In healthy relationships, each person has a sense of personal power. We read in 2 Timothy 1:7, "For God hath not given us a spirit of fear; but of power and of love and of a sound mind." This verse makes it clear that a sense of personal power precedes love and leads to a sound mind. Without a sense of personal power, we are condemned to live in fear. Interestingly, women whose incorrect understanding of submission [allowing themselves to be controlled] requires them to be powerless…live in a constant state of generalized anxiety.[7]

When a couple pledges to empower each other rather than control each other, "instead of the thornbush will grow the pine tree, and instead of briers the myrtle will grow" (Isaiah 55:13).

During the writing of this chapter, I caught myself trying to make a controlling call in a decision only my husband should make. He is in the process of starting a home-based business, and he needed a receipt book. He mentioned that after the children went to sleep he was going to go to Wal-Mart. I told him that our computer has a receipt program, and we could print out a receipt.

"No," he said casually. "I really want a receipt book."

I couldn't see the beauty of his driving to Wal-Mart at 10:30 at night. I hated for him to have to go because he was absolutely exhausted. I mean, what's the deal?

I opened my mouth to once again try to persuade him to see things my way—then I shut it and mumbled something about writing a chapter on control. Next, I gave myself a brief yet potent lecture that went something like this:

Self, if he wants to go to Wal-Mart at 10:30 at night then that's his choice. This is his business, for Pete's sake! He gives you the freedom to run your home business the way you prefer, now give him the same freedom. He is a grown man!...Yes, and what a man he is!

Any time a woman tries to control her husband, she is undermining the qualities she initially found attractive and compromising the adventurous possibilities of a romantic marriage. Releasing our husbands to God, irrevocably and completely, is a gateway to truly enjoying them and savoring their masculinity.

> *However it is debased or misinterpreted, love is a redemptive feature. To focus on one individual so that their desires become superior to yours is a very cleansing experience.*
>
> JEANETTE WINTERSON

Love-Based Marriages

When addressing issues of marital relationships, it's vital that our focus on key verses also includes an examination of the Bible's other teachings. According to Christ, every law written and every prophet's message all center upon one concept: "So in everything, do to others what you would have them do to you, for this sums up the Law and the Prophets" (Matthew 7:12). Jesus didn't say this applies to everything except marriage. He said this concept applies to all of life—and that includes marriage. Any marital concept that is taught without alignment to the "do unto others" philosophy is contrary to God's general plan for life and marriage.

> *A new command I give you: Love one another. As I have loved you, so you must love one another.*

By this all men will know that you are my disciples,
if you love one another.

JOHN 13:34

The husband and wife who are putting into practice Matthew 7:12 are free of the need to control one another. Free in their security. Free in their mutual respect and submission. Free in their love and joy. Free to savor great sex and heightened romance. Let's look at the contrast between control-based and love-based relationships.

- *A control-based marriage believes God is sovereign first.*

- *A love-based marriage believes God is love first.*

People who view God as a dictator usually believe they have a God-given right to rule over others. This thought process says, "If we are to be Christlike, and Christ was God, then we are like Him when we seize control." The only problem with this is that spouses who want to take control don't want their spouses to dictate to them. This concept is in direct contrast to "do to others what you would have them do to you" (see Matthew 7:12).

> Whoever does not love does not know God, because God is love (1 John 4:8).

> If we love one another, God lives in us and his love is made complete in us (1 John 4:12).

> And so we know and rely on the love God has for us. God is love. Whoever lives in love lives in God, and God in him....There is no fear in love. But perfect love drives out

fear, because fear has to do with punishment. The one who fears is not made perfect in love (1 John 4:16,18).

ᶜ *A control-based marriage is centered around an individual.*

ᶜ *A love-based marriage is Christ-centered and, therefore, focuses on meeting the needs of and serving the other spouse.*

A controller is more interested in what he or she wants than in what the other person wants. A controller can also never be completely committed to the Lord or completely God-focused because that person is too centered upon getting his or her own way. A control-based marriage will be like "oil and water." The two people cannot be one because one person is refusing to relinquish his or her desires to dominate and control the other one.

Love is not self-seeking (1 Corinthians 13:5).

In the beginning was the Word, and the Word was with God, and the Word was God. He was with God in the beginning. Through him all things were made; without him nothing was made that has been made. In him was life, and that life was the light of men. The light shines in the darkness, but the darkness has not understood it (John 1:1-5).

ᶜ *A control-based marriage focuses on only a few Scriptures and ignores significant passages.*

ᶜ *A love-based marriage looks to the whole Bible for guidance on healthy relationships, and both partners look to Jesus Christ for light and direction.*

A control-based marriage essentially uses the Bible as a means to constrain rather than a way to spiritual enlightenment. Narrow theories are developed while turning a blind eye to Scriptures that contradict the practice or at least bring it into balance. For instance, decades ago some men thought the Ephesians 5–6 passage on submission gave them the God-ordained right to beat their wives and own slaves. The legal system supported their view. Today, some men believe that the same passage gives them unlimited power over their spouses, even to the point of verbal abuse and condescension, which often carries over to women in general.

> When Jesus spoke again to the people, he said, "I am the light of the world. Whoever follows me will never walk in darkness, but will have the light of life" (John 8:12).

> As a prisoner for the Lord, then, I urge you to live a life worthy of the calling you have received. Be completely humble and gentle; be patient, bearing with one another in love. Make every effort to keep the unity of the Spirit through the bond of peace (Ephesians 4:1-3).

> ❧ *A control-based marriage exists by a rigid list of do's & don'ts that deal with external life and behavior.*

> ❧ *A love-based marriage thrives upon the Christlike love spilling from the internal spirit of both spouses.*

> When true Christlike love invades the hearts of both spouses, each spouse is so concentrated on meeting the other's needs that no one has the time to "keep score." Nonetheless, each spouse finds ultimate fulfillment in his or her needs being met and in pouring themselves out for the other. In such a marriage, neither party is standing back with arms folded, refusing to rise to a specific task.

Rather, the two pitch in as one on all fronts and work together as one unit.

The man said, "This is now bone of my bones and flesh of my flesh; she shall be called 'woman,' for she was taken out of man." For this reason a man will leave his father and mother and be united to his wife, and they will become one flesh (Genesis 2:23,24).

For he who loves his fellow man [or spouse] has fulfilled the law....Love does no harm to its neighbor [or spouse]. Therefore love is the fulfillment of the law (Romans 13:8,10).

♭ *A control-based marriage breeds resentment and fear.*

♭ *A love-based marriage breeds openness and respect.*

Many people who are the victims of controllers will hide purchases, activities, and thoughts to protect themselves and give them areas of "control" in their lives. A victim of control will never completely trust the controller. His or her heart will be hidden deep inside, and the controller will never hold that person's true respect or honor.

I am my lover's and my lover is mine (Song of Songs 6:3).

♭ *In a control-based marriage, couple decisions are made by one party with little or no regard to the effect on the other spouse.*

♭ *In a love-based marriage, couple decisions are made jointly and to the benefit of the family. Or a joint decision is made to delegate specific decisions to a spouse in his or her area of expertise or giftedness.*

In a control-based marriage, the controlled party usually is convinced that he or she has no right to participate in the decision-making process. This might stem from a limited view of Scripture or from an undermining of the victim's self-confidence. If the victim believes he or she has a right to participate in decision-making but is habitually ignored, then the controlled person will struggle with resentment and frustration. The subjugated partner will usually carve out areas where he or she can make decisions and then hide the products of the decisions.

"In a study of couples, Pepper Schwartz, author of *Peer Marriage,* found that among couples who enjoy equality in their marriages, there's less of the rank-pulling and power-playing so often seen in unhappy unions. Schwartz reports that these egalitarian twosomes have conversations filled with what she calls 'tag questions,' such as 'Do you agree?' and 'What do you think?'"[8] If a Christ-centered couple cannot come to a consensus, they seek God together until they receive divine direction.

> God does not show favoritism (Acts 10:34).

> The body is a unit, though it is made up of many parts; and though all its parts are many, they form one body. So it is with Christ. For we were all baptized by one Spirit into one body—whether Jews or Greeks, slave or free—and we were all given the one Spirit to drink (1 Corinthians 12:12,13).

We have different gifts, according to the grace given us....Be devoted to one another in brotherly love. Honor one another above yourselves (Romans 12:6,10).

> ♭ *In a control-based marriage, a husband controller is sexually frustrated.*

℘ *In a love-based marriage, the husband is sexually pleased.*

The wife of a controller might have sex with him, but she cannot release her heart to him because she has walled it up for protection. Even though one human may have external control over another, he or she will never possess the other person's pure adoration. This results in an either less-than-exciting sex life or infrequent sex. A wife who feels controlled will, for the most part, not enjoy sex and will often turn down her husband's advances. Also, a controlling husband might find that his wife turns the tables on him and uses sex as a reward/punishment tool.

> My dove in the clefts of the rock, in the hiding places on the mountainside, show me your face, let me hear your voice; for your voice is sweet, and your face is lovely (Song of Songs 2:14).

℘ *In a control-based marriage, a wife controller uses sex as manipulation.*

℘ *In a love-based marriage, a wife strives to meet her husband's sexual needs.*

A controlling wife seeks areas where she can get her way. Often she recognizes her husband's deep need for sex and uses that against him. This creates a less-than-exciting sex life because it will always be overshadowed by issues of control. It undermines a man's masculinity and strength of will because he becomes a beggar.

> Listen! My lover! Look! Here he comes, leaping across the mountains, bounding over the hills. My lover is like a gazelle or a young stag. Look! There he stands behind our wall, gazing through the windows, peering through the lattice. My lover spoke and said to me, "Arise, my darling,

my beautiful one, and come with me" (Song of Songs 2:8-10).

ᚦ *In a control-based marriage, chauvinism often permeates the marriage.*

ᚦ *In a love-based marriage, both husband and wife appreciate that they were created in the image of God.*

A controller looks down upon the controlled party, often due to gender issues. If a woman believes her husband is a "helpless man," she will override his every move. If a man believes his wife is a "stupid female," he will never allow her to make important decisions on her own. When people condescend the opposite sex, they are condescending God because Genesis 1 states that *men and women were created in God's image.*

So God created man in his own image, in the image of God he created him; male and female he created them (Genesis 1:27).

However, each one of you also must love his wife as he loves himself, and the wife must respect her husband (Ephesians 5:33).

If you recognize your marriage in the previous descriptions of control-based marriages, dare to begin the journey of repair. The first step is to be honest with yourself and your spouse. If you are a controller, ask God to forgive you. Next, release your life and your spouse to the Lord. Have faith in God's wisdom, and trust Him to work out your life and your relationships for your good. Then ask your spouse to forgive you. If he will, ask him to pray aloud for you. Be noble enough to allow your spouse to comment when you are slipping into the old patterns, then correct yourself. This process takes ample doses of courage and, most likely, long nights on your knees before God. But the freedom you find in your marriage will take your breath away.

If your spouse is a controller, realize that belligerence on your part will only make matters worse. And silence will only enable the controller and entrench negative patterns. What can you do? Pray for your spouse that he will see his erroneous ways. It may take a year or two of consistent prayer, but know that God honors the prayers of a noble, godly woman. Gently and lovingly share with your husband that his control is shriveling your love for him. You might need to humbly share the same message with him on six or more occasions over a period of time before you are truly communicating with him. Ask him to read this chapter. Continue to meet his sexual needs and try your best to be an excellent wife. Remember, once he sees you hurling yourself into meeting his sexual needs, he will very likely ask how he can serve you in return. If appropriate, go to a Christian marriage counselor who promotes Bible-based, *balanced* marriages that honor both husband and wife.

Reality Checks

Cultural

Ironically, we often experience love-based courtships then control-based marriages. I think this is one of the huge disillusionments of many marriages. It's almost like a soft cry that is never spoken, the essence of "but I thought you said you loved me." Sometimes people know deep in their hearts that a control-based marriage is less than fulfilling, but they cannot imagine another way. Don't be surprised if breaking free of this pattern takes several years. Many couples fall into this trap—and once they're in it few break free. *Be one of the few!* Dare to truly become one.

Spiritual

Don't expect to break the patterns of control without becoming a prayer warrior. This is where the "rubber meets the road" in marriages. A controller will only find deliverance through abandonment to God. A person set on controlling a spouse has yet to relinquish all his or her heart to the Lord. There's a depth in spiritual existence that many refuse to plumb. It only comes to a person who commits to hours a week in prayer, whose heart is abandoned to the will of God, and who devours the Word of God. Such a heart will find freedom from the need to control others or will experience the grace to endure while a controlling spouse awakens to the needs of a biblically based marriage.

Real Life

If your husband is a controller, you might wonder if he will go to his grave still trying to control you. Hopefully, he will listen to your cries for change. Hopefully, he will heed the voice of the Lord. But there are no guarantees. God gave Adam and Eve a choice in the Garden of Eden, and He still gives people choices today. Choose to persevere in loving, respecting, and praying for your husband. More than one woman has seen a miraculous turnaround to a marriage she thought was beyond repair.

Prayer Points for Freedom

If you are struggling with issues of control, the following suggestions will begin your journey to relational freedom.

- ♭ Pray that God will purge your heart of the need to be in control.

- ♭ Pray that the Lord will deliver you from the fear that most likely underlies your need to control.

- Pray that the Lord will reveal the source of that fear to you.

- Pray for the spiritual strength to confess your sin to your mate and begin forging a new relationship together.

- If your spouse is a controller, release him to God, then pray these points for him as well.

- Pray that you will have the courage to lovingly be honest with your mate about the negative patterns of your marriage.

Romantic Notions

How beautiful you are, my darling! Oh, how beautiful!
Your eyes behind your veil are doves. Your hair is like a
flock of goats descending from Mount Gilead.
Your teeth are like a flock of sheep just shorn,
coming up from the washing.
Each has its twin; not one of them is alone.
Your lips are like a scarlet ribbon; your mouth is lovely.

SONG OF SONGS 4:1-3

What I Did

We attend a small church in a rural town. Every Sunday night after church, almost the whole congregation goes to Dairy Queen. This particular Sunday evening, our two children wound up riding with the pastor's family. As Daniel and I pulled into the Dairy Queen parking lot, I thought, *I oughta just kidnap Daniel for about five minutes and lay a kiss on him he won't soon forget.* So I drove all the way around the restaurant and back onto the highway. After I pulled into a shadowed, secluded parking lot, I grabbed him by the front of his shirt, tugged him toward me, and wowed him with a kiss that knocked his socks off.

My Reason

This created a sense of suspense and expectancy—even if it was only for five minutes. Daniel didn't know what I was up to, and I refused to tell him. Since I was driving the van, I was the one "in control." This was one time when control was sexy, fun, and mischievous!

How I Felt

Rather clever.

The Obstacles I Overcame

I did have a flash of, *Will the church family notice we are late and wonder what happened?* Then I decided that would be okay. As things turned out, no one suspected a thing.

My Husband's Response

At first he said, "What are you doing? Where are we going?" I just grinned and kept driving. By the time we stopped and I grabbed his shirt, he was smiling big. When the kiss was over, he said something to the effect of, "Yes!"

What I Wish I Had Done

This was one of those moments that's just about regret free. I didn't plan on doing this; it just happened. My only regret is that I didn't turn into a kissing kidnapper years ago.

Budget Suggestions

I have no idea how much gas it took to drive to the next parking lot—maybe 25 cents!

7

Surviving the Storms

*Hatred stirs up dissension,
but love covers over all wrongs.*

PROVERBS 10:12

IN 19 YEARS OF MARRIAGE, MY HUSBAND AND I have had our allotment of conflicts. Frankly, some of them have resembled a verbal Armageddon. In our early years of marriage, we were pretty much like everybody else. We shared enough interpersonal conflict to hold seething resentments against each other that could plague us even now if we so chose. There were also many times a conflict didn't happen because one or the other of us stuffed our emotions and bit our tongues. We have given each other grief.

A fact of life is that in every marriage conflict is going to happen. The less spiritually and emotionally mature the husband and wife, the greater the potential for conflict. What have your conflicts been over? I'm sure you have recognized that there are 1. conflicts; 2. Conflicts; 3. *Conflicts*; 4. *Conflicts*; and then there are 5. *!Conflicts!*

1. conflicts. These are the tiny issues that get under your skin. For example, dirty socks. What is the deal with men and dirty socks? No matter what the man does for a living, whether a janitor or a doctor, most leave their dirty socks lying around. It's almost like a rite of male passage. I would not be surprised to learn that fathers pull sons aside before they get married and say, "Okay, the number-one thing you need to remember is to leave your dirty

socks lying around the house." (If your husband is not a victim of dirty sock syndrome, then please substitute whatever that little thing is that aggravates you.)

There was a time in my marriage when I would go around the house picking up Daniel's dirty socks. I would fume, "Why in the world a grown man can't pick up his own socks is beyond me! What in the name of common sense would it take for him to just pick up his own socks? I've got enough to do without picking up after him!"

But that was before I fell head over heels in love with my own husband. When I truly fell in love with him—the kind of unconditional love discussed in chapter 2—the dirty socks no longer bothered me. They blessed me! I know at this point you probably think I have lost my marbles. I haven't! I've lost my heart! I've lost it to the most wonderful man alive. And I am truly honored to pick up his dirty socks. Without dirty socks, I wouldn't have my man. Those socks are evidence that I've got a great husband, and I am now honored to complete him by picking up the socks. Hey, I'll even wash them by hand if that's what makes him happy!

What little thing about your husband gets under your skin? Pray that God will immerse your heart in unconditional love for your mate and that what once irritated you will now bless you!

Resolving conflicts involves allowing unconditional love to put personal idiosyncrasies in their proper perspective. Part of this is realizing that *nobody* is free of quirks. One of the things I do that my husband can't quite understand is that after I step out of my closet, I always leave the door open and the light on. Since my closet door and the bedroom door collide, Daniel is always having to turn off my closet light and shut the door. For him, it's like picking up dirty socks. But I don't leave the door open and light beaming on purpose. Never once have I thought, *I'll just leave the door ajar and the light on and it will drive him crazy. Tee hee.* For some reason, I have this pure-hearted oversight that won't go away. Unconditional love turns such conflicts into endearments.

2. Conflicts. These are arguments that spring upon every married couple, seemingly from nowhere. They are often caused by stress, anxiety, or exhaustion on the part of one spouse or both. These are the small arguments that usually evaporate once the "I'm sorrys" have been spoken. Even madly in love couples have these disagreements from time to time. Normally, they don't have any lasting harm on the relationship. Forgiveness comes easily and this type of argument often naturally resolves by bedtime. Even though my husband and I do have some thoughts about whether or not the other is from another planet during one of these tiffs, a spirit of forgiveness and love usually ends the problem.

3. *Conflicts.* These are the one-time biggies. For instance, one spouse might go against the counsel of the other in a business deal. Or you come home to find your house painted pea green and fuchsia, and you didn't even know your husband was having the job done. Many of these one-time blowups stem from pure-hearted ignorance on the part of the offender.

These type of *Conflicts* usually require a few more days to completely resolve. However, heart-to-heart sharing, along with love and a powerful spirit of forgiveness, usually brings *Conflicts* to a satisfying and definite end.

4. *Conflicts.* These are the whoppers. This type of marital problem might stem from the early years of marriage and have overtones of betrayal because a wedding vow was broken. And that doesn't necessarily mean the person committed adultery. Those vows also contain promises to respect and cherish. For instance, you find a letter your husband wrote to his former girlfriend after you were married. Even if he never mailed the letter

or saw her in person, the betrayal still exists. Or perhaps one of you had an affair. Or maybe you or your husband secretly waste large sums of money for gambling or habitually lie about finances to cover excessive spending. *Conflicts* range in degrees of seriousness from mild to extreme. For instance, if your husband wrote a woman a letter that he never mailed, it wouldn't be as deep a betrayal as if he had an affair with six women. The key to *Conflicts* is that they involve a betrayal of trust and have a way of forever shadowing a marriage. Chances are, you know what your *Conflicts* have been.

One sign that your marriage is plagued by such problems is that you live in a cycle of conflict—your marriage is more storm than delight. Every marriage is going to occasionally encounter tempests, but when they prevail continuously, you're in a negative cycle. Unresolved *Conflicts* will lead to a marriage overcome by conflicts, Conflicts, and *Conflicts*. Usually, *Conflicts* aren't discussed much. Many couples sweep these under the rug, but the emotional impact is seen when minor issues such as dirty socks and open closet doors become *huge* battlegrounds. After years of ignoring significant issues, a couple may not be able to "see" each other because of the mound between them. At this point many couples file for divorce.

Part of the remedy for these *Conflicts* is to break the cycle of silence and deal with them one at a time. If you begin developing intimacy with God, He will bring these issues up one at a time. When you have a recurring thought—during prayer and during the day—that is in agreement with Scripture, you'll know God is communicating with you. It might be that He will require you to exercise unconditional love and walk through forgiveness for your mate. It may be that your mate will need to do the same. It is not God's will for a couple to live their lives with such issues blocking their love. Begin to pray today that your marriage will be freed from the bondage of these types of *Conflicts*.

5. *!Conflicts!* These issues usually involve physical or sexual abuse and severe verbal, emotional, or spiritual abuse. If this is what you're experiencing, read *Angry Men and the Women Who Love Them* by Paul Hegstrom (Beacon Hill Press, 1999). He was a wife abuser and adulterer whom God delivered from the cycle of abuse. He and his wife now enjoy a solid, healthy marriage. Hegstrom covers the gamut of abuse then offers hope and courage to those caught in these marriage situations. If you have experienced any kind of abuse, this book will give you the courage to call the police and seek refuge. It also affirms that God is in the business of healing relationships and delivering families from cycles of pain.

Even if your marriage has been free of brutality, I recommend that you read *Angry Men and the Women Who Love Them*. Hegstrom's message made me appreciate the man I have. After reading the book, I was so overcome with respect and love for my husband that I grabbed him and kissed his whole face. Furthermore, I am more determined to continue to put conflicts in their proper perspective and take care of them before they escalate.

"When a couple is not getting along and experiences conflicts that need to be resolved, both [partners] must recognize that the value of the relationship is greater than the conflict at hand. A primary tool in conflict resolution is to identify the problem and *together* attack the problem instead of each other."[1] Proverbs 10:12 NASB says, "Hatred stirs up strife, but love covers all sins." God's unconditional love looks past the conflict to the heart of the spouse. Don't forget that the number-one need for both a man and a woman in marriage is unconditional love.[2] This type of love doesn't seek to prove it was right at the cost of the relationship or attempt to control or manipulate. True love lays down its life for the other person. While committed spouses admit they would die for each other, it's just as important that they allow God to empower them to emanate His love, live for Him, and live for each other.   ·

There are many in the world who are dying
for a piece of bread but there are many more dying for a little love.
The poverty in the West is a different kind of poverty—it is not
only a poverty of loneliness but also
a poverty of spirituality. There's a hunger for love,
as there is a hunger for God.

MOTHER TERESA

I'm convinced that Christ's healing comes primarily through *taking the time to embrace His love.* We use the word "love" so loosely in our culture that it has almost lost depth of meaning. So when we start talking about God's love, we tend to think it is not much more potent than the shallow emotion that is so cheaply thrown around today. In reality, the love of God is beyond human knowledge, ability, or experience. Therefore, when we take the time—several hours a week—to sit and embrace that love, we unleash a force of healing in our hearts, our marriages, and our homes that leaves us speechless with its power.

Just as Christ died on the cross to free us of the bondage of sin, so His death has the power to deliver our marriages from the curse of the past. Many times, past conflicts and turmoil haunt a marriage for the whole marriage. But life doesn't have to be that way. Regardless of what your past includes, Jesus Christ can and will empower you, then heal your soul and the spirit of your marriage.

What unresolved conflicts lie beneath the surface of your marriage? Whatever they are, it is my hope that the following true story about a marriage that held together against all odds will give you courage to face your past mistakes, forgive, and move forward to a bright future in the Lord.

A *Marriage that Survived*
by Erica Meiers*

I have a wonderful marriage to a truly wonderful man; however, it hasn't always been like this. Just before our fifth anniversary, my husband confessed that he had previously had three affairs over the course of those five years and that he wanted to start dating another woman.

I packed Ray's things and walked with him to his car. At that time, I was pregnant with our third child. In the state I lived in, a couple wasn't allowed to divorce when the wife was pregnant, so I wasn't able to do anything for a few months. Even though I was not yet a Christian, I knew God could heal my marriage.

I prayed every day that God would open my husband's eyes so that he could see what he was doing and that he would understand what he was throwing away. Of course, my prayers also were for myself, that I would be able to just "live." I was devastated. I did the seesaw thing with my emotions. One day I hated my husband. How could he do that to me? It wasn't fair! Then I'd cry and cry because I loved him so much and couldn't stand the thought of living without him. Over the next couple of months, I learned to rely on God for my happiness (which, quite honestly, there wasn't much of) and my strength. I even began to look to God for meaning in my life. I prayed every day and read my Bible.

Approximately two months after my husband left me, our baby was due. We found out that I was going to have to have a cesarean section. My husband wanted to be there for us during my recovery. Although I wasn't sure it was the best thing to do, I let him move back in to help with our little boys. During the two weeks of my recovery, he decided he really didn't want to throw away our marriage. He went to a friend's pastor and told him everything. Then he prayed to receive Jesus as his Lord and Savior.

---

* The names and some situations have been changed to protect the privacy of the people involved.

After talking with me about it, I went to church and did the same. We became Christians within a few days of one another. This was probably the happiest time of my life! My husband and I decided to work on our marriage. We knew that with God's help and our determination we could get past our past.

But I was also given a genuine desire to see the other women saved. Since I had just gotten saved myself, I was so sure God could solve all their problems if they would just let Him. But soon I found the women coming to mind often. When they did, my thoughts changed from wanting their salvation to a tormenting obsession. I'd think of them with Ray. I'd think of Ray with them. I'd think of things they had said to me and how they all pretended they were my friends while sleeping with my husband. I'd have these awful feelings swell up inside, and I'd begin to hate Ray all over again. Many times he'd come home from work, and I'd be so angry with him—and he had no idea why. I had nightmares, and my daydreams ran wild with thoughts of what they did when they were together.

I finally couldn't take the torment anymore and spoke with my pastor. He told me he thought Satan was bringing them to mind to keep me stirred up. He suggested that rather than allowing the thoughts to grow and keep me tortured, I start praying for these women every time I thought of them, and eventually Satan would stop reminding me of them. Satan obviously didn't want me to pray for their salvation. My pastor thought that God would have me forgive them and put them in His hands, and that He'd have some other believer pray for them—someone who hadn't been hurt by them the way I had.

I actively forgave them after that. Every time I thought of them, I would tell God that I forgave them and ask Him to send someone into their paths who would be able to reach them with the message of salvation. It took a couple of months, but eventually I rarely thought of them. And when I did it was almost unemotional. I didn't hurt when thoughts of them arose.

Eventually, everything settled back down. Ray even quit his job because it wasn't conducive to healthy family life. He took another job that was supposed to provide him with more time at home. We attended church together, spent every evening together, did more things as a family. I believe it was easy for me to forgive him because I had just been forgiven all my sins, and I was sure that God would always be first in both our lives —and that there would never, ever be any more affairs.

I began to feel God's tug on my heart to become more involved in true worship. I began to worship all day, every day. I'd sing and pray while I was washing dishes, vacuuming floors, cleaning bathrooms. My children and I would go around the house singing praise songs to the Lord. God became my focus. I read my Bible during the boys' nap time. I would put them to bed and turn on a worship tape and sing and pray while I folded laundry. I'd finish the housework and get on my knees in the dark living room and pour my heart out to God. I grew spiritually by leaps and bounds. God was daily taking me closer to the place in Him where I would be able to stand through all the mess that He knew was soon to happen....

I have to stop right here, though, and say that God didn't cause the negative situation. It was never His fault. If you are in a situation similar to mine, please don't fall into the trap of blaming God. Yes, God knew that it was going to happen, but no, He didn't cause it. Looking back to the things that led up to this era of our lives, I can clearly see God trying to lead and direct us to prevent this very thing from happening.

During this time, my husband took another job. He was in training away from home for longer than any man should have to be away from his family. He began to lose touch with us. Ray still loved us very much and missed us like crazy, but in the everyday things, we weren't there. He gradually began to adjust to that. When his job required many hours of work, it was easier to stay and work than to come home and get reacquainted with all of us.

He began to work from 8:00 A.M. to midnight or later, even on the days he was supposed to be off. Before long, he was missing church every Wednesday and every Sunday. Finally, he even quit trying to go to church. He'd just stay at work. Then he started counseling a woman he worked with who was having trouble in her marriage. This led to the two of them developing a friendship, which in turn developed into much more than that.

At first, I only knew that he no longer wanted to go to church. I didn't know he was having an affair. I prayed for him all the time, and I asked other church members to pray for him. So many people were holding him before God every day that he didn't stand a chance!

One Sunday evening, during the praise and worship time in our service, I was standing and singing when suddenly I had a mental vision. I saw my husband in a very dark place. It was utter darkness. From the right corner, I heard a voice in my mind say, "The power of the enemy is broken in Ray's life. I declare the power of the enemy is now broken in Ray's life. The enemy is now defeated in Ray's life. The enemy no longer has any power in Ray's life." These statements were repeated several times.

Then I saw my husband surrounded by the enemy. They were in a circle around him so tight that you couldn't have passed a piece of paper between their shoulders. I saw bodies only. They weren't as tall as Ray, who is six feet, but maybe a little stockier. Mostly what I saw was the darkness that surrounded them. The scene made a real impression on me because of the complete darkness. Still, I could see Ray and the others clearly.

I remember seeing colors and images, but the darkness and the voice I heard stand out the most. The voice seemed to come from a spot in the upper right corner of the darkness. When the voice was heard, the enemy toppled in the same direction like dominoes, all the way around the circle. Next they just disappeared. Then chains and ropes and shackles fell to the "floor" around Ray's feet and disappeared. I began to weep. I knew that I had just heard the Lord speak. I was shaken, but excited. God was doing something magnificent in my husband's life. At that point, I only knew he was drifting from the Lord. I shared what had happened with the whole church right then and asked them to not stop praying for him.

The next morning I called my best friend in another state. While I was in the middle of telling her what had happened, I heard the Lord speak again. He said, "The latter glory will be greater than the former glory in Ray's relationship with me." I was stunned. To have a vision was awesome in itself, but then to actually hear God speak...I was unable to talk for several minutes. (I have never had another vision, and I have only heard God's voice like that one other time.)

During the next few months, things began to grow worse and worse between my husband and me. I began to see signs in his actions toward me that pointed to him being unfaithful. He never wanted to be intimate. He'd stay at work really late. He wouldn't be where he was supposed to be, and it would be quite some time before he finally got my messages. He'd be really impatient with me if I asked what his plans were for a particular day. He would never be home when he said he would be. If I asked what kept him, he'd get mad. Times when he used to be gentle with me or tease me about something, he was now either indifferent or impatient. I remember on New Year's Eve he told me he'd be home before midnight so we could celebrate the new year together. Finally, at 3:30 A.M., after not being able to reach him at work where he was supposed to be, I called the police and asked them to stop by the restaurant where he worked and check on him. They called back and told me the place was dark and all locked up. Nobody was there. Finally, about two hours later, Ray came home. He denied the accusation that he was having an affair.

Even in the face of all these signs, I didn't want to believe that Ray was involved with another woman. One day, the other woman's husband openly accused my husband of being involved with his wife. Ray denied it, saying that the guy was upset that they were getting a divorce and he was looking for someone to accuse. I chose to believe my husband. After all, we were Christians.

After that, almost every time I read my Bible a verse would speak very clearly to me. Usually they were verses that gave me hope and strength. The passage that was the most special to me at that time was Romans 4:18,20,21. I'll share it with you the way the Holy Spirit showed it to me: "Against all hope, [Erica] in hope believed....Yet [she] did not waver through unbelief regarding the promise of God, but was strengthened in [her] faith and gave glory to God, being fully persuaded that God had power to do what he had promised." My "promise" was the vision God had given me. I believed God meant what He said. Somehow, deep inside, I knew the situation was going to get worse before it got better. God was showing me how to stand in Him so the waves of adversity couldn't toss me around.

Many other things happened during the time that followed, and God revealed much to me through the reading of His Word. One of the most significant truths came when I was praying one night. This was the only other time I have literally heard God's voice speak to me. I had prayed and cried and prayed some more, then finally quieted down and rested in God's presence. All of a sudden I heard Him say, "You can pray for Ray with the same authority and confidence you pray for yourself because you are one flesh." It was a turning point in my life.

Up until that moment, I was always afraid to pray for Ray because I really wasn't sure what God's will was and I didn't know how far I should go in praying. I didn't want to assume anything in my prayers, so I was really cautious. But from that time on, my prayers changed drastically. I took a stand against the enemy. By this point I was no longer sure if Ray was being honest with me, but I knew he was definitely under attack from the enemy. I began to stand in Ray's place in spiritual battle against the forces of darkness. I can tell you right now, I've never been as bold as I was then.

Almost one month later, I called my friend and asked her to pray for me that day. I knew deep inside that Ray was going to tell me everything. I suddenly accepted that he was having an affair, and I was ready to face it. About two hours later, he called me from work and asked if I'd be free in a little bit because he wanted to talk to me. When he came home, he told me everything, then asked me what I wanted him to do. I told him he needed to face the consequences of his actions, and I'd have his things packed for him after the boys went to bed that night.

After that things are blurry. I had felt that God was telling me to get a legal separation. I won't begin to guess why, except that maybe Ray needed something to open his eyes. But I didn't file for a legal separation; I filed for divorce. I'll never know how God had planned to work because I didn't do what I knew in my heart I was being told to do. I took the easy way out; I did it my way. I often wonder what would have happened differently if I had obeyed to the letter, instead of just a little bit.

Once I made my decision, I went to the lawyer's office to sign the divorce papers on a Monday. The following Wednesday the kids and I packed a couple of suitcases and drove to Mom's. She put us up for the week so I could look for a job and a place to live. On Sunday Ray called. Only a week lapsed from the day I signed the papers to the day he called. He told me he couldn't stay with his girlfriend anymore. He just couldn't continue in that relationship. He asked for an opportunity to talk things over with me.

My but I was surprised! I didn't expect God to work that fast. I wasn't sure if I even *wanted* to let God work in our marriage at that point. Even after all my praying and committing, I was really hurting. I didn't want to take the chance the same thing would happen again. The first affairs happened before we turned our lives over to God, but this time the infidelity occurred while we were Christians. There was no guarantee that Ray wouldn't break our wedding vows again. I was scared of being hurt, but I knew God really wanted me to keep trying.

I stayed at Mom's until the next Thursday. I went back home and, after work, Ray came over to talk. Actually, he talked a little and then listened while I took all my pain and frustration out on him. He was so humble. He sat there and took it. He apologized over and over. He said to me at one point that he didn't know what else to do except apologize. He couldn't undo what he'd done, but he wanted to try to make things right again.

A battle was raging in my mind and in my heart. I wanted so much to make him hurt as much as he'd hurt me, but I also wanted to let God do what He wanted in our lives. I sat precariously on the fence between forgiveness and retaliation for most of the night. But God had become so close to me over the previous months that I couldn't turn my back on Him. I had to give Ray another chance. I had to forgive him. Not because I wanted to, but because *God* wanted me to. I had to honor God in my marriage.

It took many months before trusting Ray became natural again. As a matter of fact, the hardest times were only beginning. After everything was brought out in the open, Ray lost his job for fraternizing with an employee. Then the other husband began following him home after work at night. He'd slash two tires on our car every night. I believe it was by the grace of God that we had two spares, and the guy never slashed three tires. I've never put so many used tires on a car in my lifetime! I became afraid for our safety. I knew the other man carried a gun with him, and many times Ray would have to drive from work to the police station to get him to quit following him. I was afraid to let the boys play outside for fear the other man would shoot one of them to hurt Ray. This situation kept all the pain right up front and out in the open for a long, long time.

Ray and I began to pray together for the first time, and we attended marriage classes to work through our problems. We started dating one another every week. Tuesday was our "date night." We made this commitment to each other, and nothing else took priority over that. Ray told his employer that under no circumstances could he work on Tuesday nights, and he was honest about the reasons why. His employer honored his forthrightness and never asked him to work those nights.

All our troubles weren't over, though. I still had to learn to really trust Ray. I had chosen to forgive him, and I had to keep reminding myself of it every day for months. Trust doesn't happen because we forgive. Just as forgiveness is a choice, so is trust. I had many opportunities to wonder if Ray was being faithful, but each time I had to choose to believe he was. I prayed many times that God would help me not assume Ray was out with a woman when he was a little late getting home.

I learned then, too, that if I showed trust in Ray, he proved to be more trustworthy. When I'd get upset about him being late and start sarcastically asking whom he was with, he'd begin to lose hope that things could be right between us. He realized he had to reearn my trust, but I also had to show him I was willing to try again. Ray knew he'd been wrong and that he'd hurt me, but now he was trying to be the husband he was supposed to be. It would frustrate and hurt him when I'd bring up his infidelities.

It has now been six years since Ray's last affair. His relationship with God is better than ever. Our relationship as husband and wife grows stronger each week.

A good marriage doesn't just happen. It takes work and commitment. A couple must decide to stay together and work no matter how hard life gets. I learned that adultery is one of the hardest things a couple could ever deal with. But in God's eyes, adultry is a sin like any other sin. God classifies every transgression in the same category...sin. Jesus died to provide forgiveness for our sins. Ray hurt me when he had affairs, but I discovered through his deeds that I had been unfaithful to Jesus. Anytime I don't obey when I know God wants me to do something, I'm being unfaithful. Anytime I put another person or activity before God or my relationship with Him, I'm being unfaithful. Jesus hurts when I'm unfaithful, just as I hurt when Ray was unfaithful. Who am I to say that I won't forgive Ray for his wrongdoing, when I expect to be forgiven for mine?

Many women might think it would be easier to get rid of men like Ray. After all, the Bible does allow for divorce in the case of fornication or adultery. But would a divorced life really be better? I can attest to the fact that many times I'd look at other men in the church and think, *He'd never do what Ray did. I wish I had a husband like him.* But I learned that one of the men I had assumed would never even look at a woman other than his wife wanted our church to address the issue of adultery and remaining faithful. I had thought he'd never be one to struggle in that area. No one is free from temptation. Don't trade your husband in on the chance you'll get one who doesn't make mistakes.

God is truly able to bring good out of the pain and hurt you're facing. He may not give you a vision; He may not speak to you like He did to me. But He will walk with you, and many times He'll carry you through situations you come up against. He won't leave you alone; He will draw you closer to Him. It's up to you to take the steps He's asking of you. He wants to hide you under the shadow of His wings and give you the strength to stand with Him through all your pain. But you can't have a pity party when God doesn't make everything perfect overnight. Life is a journey—a journey that causes you to grow and mature. Walking the path of forgiveness will stretch and strengthen you if you'll let it.

Forgiveness and trust are a choice. No one can earn forgiveness; it has to be given freely. Pray until you are able to truly forgive. Choose to trust. When you feel bitterness and anger flare up, pray. Release those feelings to the Lord, and ask Him to help you. He will give you the ability to forgive and trust again.

> *Place me like a seal over your heart,*
> *like a seal on your arm; for love is as strong as death, its jealousy*
> *unyielding as the grave. It burns like blazing fire, like a mighty*
> *flame. Many waters cannot quench love; rivers cannot wash it*
> *away. If one were to give all the wealth of his house for love, it*
> *would be utterly scorned.*
>
> SONGS OF SONGS 8:6,7

Reality Checks

The Facts of Marriage

If you are thinking of leaving your husband, realize that even another marriage with another man stands the chance of unraveling. When you divorce one man and marry another, you are essentially ripping your soul in half and then attempting to merge it with another. The wounds take years to heal, and the likelihood of a second-marriage divorce is much greater than that of a first-marriage divorce. We fool ourselves when we believe we are going to find "Mr. Wonderful" and blend our families into one big, happy unit with very little struggle. "The Brady Bunch" seldom exists in the real world. I encourage you to take every healthy, God-ordained measure you have available to make your marriage work. *Never* enable sin or selfishness, but *do* live Christ with every fiber of your being!

The Facts of Children

If you have children and think a divorce will not affect them that much, please think again. My own parents divorced, and I speak from personal experience. Divorce is an emotional abortion that will devastate your children. While I don't believe a woman should stay in an abusive situation or enable sin, legal separations are a great alternative to divorce in worst case scenarios. If divorce proceedings do occur, seek God long and hard to make sure you are following His leading.

The Facts of Real Life

In the real world, men divorce their wives as well. And people get divorces *then* find the Lord. There are also many bad situations that might lead to divorce for the safety of the women and children involved. If you are already divorced, take heart. If there's any way to reconcile, pray that the Lord will give you the courage to obey. But if you are in your second or third marriage, believe that while you cannot go back to your first marriage, God can and will give you a dose of His grace that will bring healing and wholeness to your past and your current marriage.*

I don't believe divorce is God's perfect will, but I do believe God takes us where we are and moves us forward. He forgives, chooses to forget, and holds us up in His amazing love.

Prayer Points for Romance

If your marriage is dying, the following prayer points will help you allow God to breathe new love into your heart and the heart of your husband.

- ✣ If you don't love your husband, pray that God will reawaken what once burned within you.

---

* For a clear presentation of the devastation of divorce tempered with God's mercy for those divorced, read my novel *Second Chances* (Harvest House, 2000). It will help you heal and give you hope.

- If you believe your marriage is beyond repair, pray that God will give you a new vision of what your marriage can be.

- Pray that God will give you the strength to do everything in your power to resurrect what He originally ordained.

- If you are struggling with forgiveness, pray that the Lord will speak to you through the next chapter.

Romantic Notions

by Erica Meiers

How beautiful on the mountains
are the feet of those who bring good news,
who proclaim peace, who bring good tidings, who proclaim salva-
tion, who say to Zion, "Your God reigns!"

ISAIAH 52:7

What I Did

While my husband was working the late shift, I traced my feet and used the patterns to cut out 40 footprints. On the first one I wrote "Follow the footprints" and taped it to the front door handle. (Of course, I waited until our boys were asleep.) I put the footprints out as though they were walking toward the living room directly to my husband's recliner. On the footprint directly in front of his chair I wrote, "Sit down, relax, enjoy a fresh Pepsi." I could have written just about anything there, but Ray's favorite beverage is Pepsi so I knew that would be the first thing he'd want after a long day at work. While he relaxed, I rubbed his shoulders and then sat and talked with him about his day. After he finished his drink, I suggested he follow those footprints to see where they led. I had placed them down the hall to the bathroom. Directly in front of the bathtub, I placed a footprint on which I had written, "Enjoy a refreshing, warm shower." While he was in the shower, I gathered up all the footprints and repositioned a few of them from the bathroom to the bedroom door. On the last footprint, the one taped to the bedroom doorknob, I wrote a special invitation for him to enter. Then I went into the bedroom, closed the door, lit the candles, changed into something romantic, and reclined on the bed while I waited for him to finish his shower. The rest is history!

My Reason

We had recently gone through a horrible time in our marriage that almost ended in divorce. I was determined that we were going to recapture the romance we had sorely lacked for quite a while.

How I Felt

I actually felt a little giddy and reckless. I was excited, but nervous that Ray would think I was silly and wouldn't cooperate with my plans. We were so recently back together that I was almost afraid of doing something to make him think I was childish.

The Obstacles I Overcame

I had to get the boys to bed quickly enough so that they'd be asleep before Ray came home from work so I'd have time to put out the feet. I also had to overcome the obstacle of my own nervousness, but I was determined that my nervousness would not stop me from doing something I thought would be good for us. In the past I was not spontaneous in matters of sexuality, but during our getting-back-together phase, I learned that Ray wanted me to be the initiator sometimes.

My Husband's Response

Ray responded exactly the way I hoped he would. After coming in the front door, he didn't hesitate to follow the path I had laid out for him. I removed his shoes, and I was rewarded with satisfied sighs as I rubbed his shoulders and feet. He drank his Pepsi a little more quickly than normal so he could see what was coming next! He had a silent question in his eyes that I refused to answer. His shower was rather brief as well. Those were the only things that were rushed that evening.

What I Wish I Had Done

That night went so perfectly, I wished I had done something like this sooner. I decided right then to be more spontaneous and not always expect him to be the one to start things. I believe men enjoy romance as much as women do!

Budget Suggestions

Because I was so rushed to get them finished, I used sheets of the boys' notebook paper. I was able to put two feet per page, so I only used about 20 sheets.

8

Pathway of Forgiveness

Forget the former things; do not dwell on the past.
See, I am doing a new thing! Now it springs up; do you not perceive it?
I am making a way in the desert and streams in the wasteland.
ISAIAH 43:18,19

IN CHAPTER 2, I MENTIONED THAT I owned two birds my husband was threatening to make into fried parakeets. Well, the birds survived, but the family agreed that my husband should arrange for the birds to have a nice, new home with one of his coworkers. Frankly, the whole family is relieved.

During the birds' tenure in our home, we often let them out of their cage. The first time I arranged for their freedom, I simply took the lid off the top of the cage and waited for them to get out. Instead of jumping to freedom, "Blue" and "Yellow" hovered near the bottom of the cage. (My children named them; I'll let you figure out what colors they were!) The birds were scared stiff. They were born in a cage and had spent their whole lives in a cage. The concept of freedom terrified them. Eventually, they scraped together the courage to hop to the top edge of the cage, teeter on the threshold of freedom, then fly around the room.

Another time, I simply opened the cage door to see what would happen. When I had taken off the top, the gateway to freedom loomed above them, large and inviting. However, hopping to freedom out the cage door required more effort on their part. Blue left the cage fairly quickly, but Yellow stayed inside. After a while, Blue realized Yellow wasn't with her. She flew back to the cage, hung on the side, and stuck her head inside the door opening. She chirped, tweeted, and encouraged Yellow to embrace freedom. However, Yellow stayed against the back of the cage and refused to take the chance of leaving the bondage she had known most of her life.

Many people are trapped in a cage—a cage of unforgiveness. And sometimes they have been in the cage for so long that when God offers them the gateway to freedom, they are terrified. They have been trapped in unforgiveness for so long that it becomes a way of life—a comfort zone. Eventually they don't even realize the bitter bile beneath the surface of their hearts is contrary to God's perfect will for His children and their marriages.

As you read this chapter, imagine that I am the blue parakeet flitting around the door of the cage of unforgiveness. Inside the cage, there is a yellow parakeet afraid to leave the bondage and soar in the grace of God. Are you by chance the yellow parakeet?

Have you, like Erica, forgiven your mate for your past *!Conflicts!?* (See chapter 7.) Have you really forgiven him? Or perhaps you are the transgressor and need your husband's forgiveness. But still, have you asked Christ to forgive you? And have you forgiven yourself?

As you search your heart over these questions, consider that forgiveness can also be thought of as the bridge between a mundane marriage and a "heavenly" marriage. Traveling from the mire of resentfulness across the bridge of forgiveness brings healing to your relationships and opens the pathway for God's mighty love and power to transform your life and your relationships. Don't be trapped in the mire of resentment your whole life and forget there's a blessed world for you to experience. In this state your marriage will most likely be bound by turmoil. But the husband and wife who have walked the path of forgiveness find themselves in a new land. A land sparkling like diamonds, reflecting the jewel of God's love. A land where freedom rules and marriage is a joy.

Even though we all want heavenly marriages, many women are like the yellow parakeet. As they stand on the hill facing the land of bliss, they gaze at the swamp between. The marsh is the dark depths in your relationship you must wade through in order to address the issues. It's easier to embrace fear and stand at the edge of the mire. Plunging into issues takes courage. Unfortunately, some people go to their graves without ever believing that God intended something miraculous in their marriages—a man and woman, both created in God's image, one in the Lord, submerged in a crystal-clear lake of love.

Do you hunger for a heavenly marriage? Are you eager to make it happen? If so, there are several characteristics to develop that will attest that you are on the path of healing and forgiving your mate and others who have harmed you. If there is an issue in your marriage or life where all of these do not apply, perhaps you are still enduring life and marriage while chained in the past.

You recognize you have not forgiven the person. Someone who is purposefully relishing thoughts of vengeance has not recognized the need to forgive. However, a person who is tempted toward vengeance but struggles against it because he or she knows retaliation doesn't speak forgiveness has recognized the need to forgive.

I have experienced forgiveness on a very deep level. It's wonderful. It's lasting. It's of God. Don't underestimate God's power to give you strength to forgive. He's ready for you to step out in faith and relinquish the whole ordeal to Him. This opens the door to breaking the bondage and experiencing freedom.

You can talk about the issues that once were so painful. This is a good indicator that you are embracing the forgiveness that leads to healing. I knew God was deepening my forgiveness and intensifying my healing regarding my sexual abuse when I had the strength to share the pain with a group of women at a shelter for the battered and abused. Two years before that, I never could have spoken the words. But God healed me to the point that He could turn my pain into the initiation of healing for others. A positive sign that true forgiveness and healing is beginning in a marriage is that the issues are no longer avoided. They are discussed, resolved, and put to rest.

You feel no need to emotionally isolate yourself from your family and friends. The cage of unforgiveness always brings isolation. Remember, Yellow stayed in her cage all day long, while Blue relished the freedom to fly. Those who are not embracing God's forgiveness and healing run from emotional intimacy with anyone, including God, and especially the person who hasn't been forgiven. If the unforgiven party is the mate, then the marriage relationship will be shallow and sex will be an act of the body alone, with no bonding of the hearts.

You have followed Jesus' words to "get up" and "take your mat." In Matthew 9:1-8, Jesus heals a paralyzed man and tells him, "Get up, take your mat and go home" (verse 6). There comes a point in our healing when we must quit wallowing in the past and allowing it to paralyze and trap us spiritually and emotionally. We can spend our whole lives in a cage reliving the pain and harboring unforgiveness. It can eventually become a barrier to all emotional and spiritual growth. While walking through the pain can take time, there comes a time to put the past behind us and allow God to make us radical influences on our marriages.

I am not minimizing the devastation of your past or the pain in your marriage. This is not a spiritual version of the cold-hearted "get over it." But neither is it a validation of harboring unforgiveness. When Jesus Christ told the man to get up and walk, He did not pull the man to his feet or pick up the mat for him. *He told the paralytic to take action.* He is also beckoning for you to take action, to enter into the freedom He offers.

You have rewritten your story. You no longer define your marriage by what has happened in the past. You view it by the present and the future Christ will give you. This also extends to wounds aside from marital conflict. You no longer define yourself by past abuse but by the fact that Jesus Christ died for you and that you are His precious child.

Read the following paragraph aloud. In your efforts to forgive, read it several times a day. Make it your spiritual motto. Type or write it out on a piece of paper and hang it on your bathroom mirror or any other highly visible locale.

> God the Father loves me so much that He stepped from eternity and broke into my world to express His love by sending His Son who sacrificed Himself to cover my sins. God did not extend Himself so I can hobble along in spiritual defeat or stay trapped in a mire or a cage, defining myself and my marriage by what has happened in the past or by what others might or might not say. Through Christ, I *will not* live in spiritual defeat. I *will not* allow Satan a foothold in my life. I *will not* hover in a cage, terrified to step through the gateway of forgiveness. I will embrace the spiritual freedom Christ offers.

> *When I was in London, I went to see*
> *the homeless people where our sisters have a*
> *soup kitchen. One man, who was living in a cardboard box, held*
> *my hand and said, "It's been a long time since I felt the warmth of*
> *a human hand."[1]*
> MOTHER TERESA

> *How long has it been since your husband*
> *felt the warmth of your hand?*
> *Not just an obligatory pat or a meaningless clasp,*
> *but the complete warmth of your hand,*
> *the warmth of your unconditional love?*

Reach out to your husband.
Hold his hand—really hold his hand.
Don't let the past destroy
your present and future.

Steps to Forgiveness

When you read through the story about the birds and the points on forgiveness, did you recognize areas in your life and marriage that might need ample doses of God's forgiveness? Most people struggle with this issue in their marriages—and in life in general. It doesn't take very long before we realize that people, even spouses, will disappoint us. *No relationship is free of the need for forgiveness,* but forgiveness is often not achieved because there is a huge gap between realizing what we must do and knowing how to implement that 11-letter word. If you are struggling with forgiveness, the following steps will empower you to move closer to the peace that will revolutionize your marriage. If your husband is struggling to forgive you, you can share this with him as well.

Perhaps the issues you struggle with lie less between you and your spouse and more with previous abuse. If so, the *Pathway of Forgiveness* will initiate your journey to healing. Take heart! As a victim of sexual abuse, I am living proof that Jesus Christ does and will heal injuries of the soul.[2] With the Holy Spirit as your guide, you *can* overcome the pain of your past. Furthermore, you and your husband can not only have a good sex life, but have an astounding one!

Pathway to Forgiveness
Step 1: Pray that God will enable you to forgive.

Forgive us our debts, as we also have forgiven our debtors….For if you forgive men when they sin against you, your heavenly Father will also forgive you. But if you do not forgive men their sins, your Father will not forgive your sins (Matthew 7:12,14,15).

A halfhearted prayer of "Lord, please help me to forgive, but let me rip out his heart first" probably won't avail that much. While honesty with God is important, there still needs to be a desire for doing what is right. When the desires of our hearts are bound up in our desires for the Lord, our ultimate goal is to please Him. Then we can focus on what His Word urges. We can forgive because we understand that He is love and that "in all things God works for the good of those who love him" (Romans 8:28).

Taking Action

The following prayers will help you in your journey.

1. If you truly cannot find a desire to forgive, then start here: "Lord, I really want to do something horrible to this person, so I need You to give me the desire to forgive." Don't use this prayer as an excuse not to forgive. If you mean this prayer, God will be faithful to fulfill your desire.

2. Be honest: "Lord, You know I'm struggling with wanting to retaliate, but my desire to please You is greater. Help!"

3. "Lord, remind me that You died for this person just like You died for me. Give me the depth of love that freely extends forgiveness."

Step 2: Ask the Lord to show you reality.

King Xerxes asked Queen Esther, "Who is he? Where is the man who has dared to do such a thing?" Esther said, "The adversary and enemy is this vile Haman." Then Haman was terrified before the king and queen. The king got up in a rage, left his wine and went out into the palace garden. But Haman, realizing that the king had already decided his fate, stayed behind to beg Queen Esther for his life (Esther 7:5-7).

Do not be deceived: God cannot be mocked. A man reaps what he sows. The one who sows to please his sinful nature, from that nature will reap destruction; the one who sows to please the Spirit, from the Spirit will reap eternal life (Galatians 6:7,8).

Search me, O God, and know my heart; test me and know my anxious thoughts. See if there is any offensive way in me, and lead me in the way everlasting (Psalm 139:23,24).

The story of Haman's plot against the Jews is an excellent example of a man whose heart was dark with the sin of pride. However, Queen Esther turned the tables on him and revealed his sin. Haman's reaction shows exactly where every perpetrator eventually lands—a prisoner of desperation because of sin. It's important to remember that all sin leads to torment and despair. Either God will make the offenders miserable with conviction or, if their consciences are seared and they don't ask forgiveness, they will meet their punishment in the afterlife.

In order to maintain an unforgiving spirit, people must believe they are something they are not—above sin. Usually an unforgiving spirit is revealed when a person says something like, "I would never…" The implication is that she (or he) is above sin, or that particular sin anyway. In reality, we all must ask the Lord to show us if there are wicked ways in us. In order to follow Christ, we must come to a point of asking Him to forgive us. Once we get a picture of ourselves at the base of the cross, holding a hammer in our hands, with Jesus' blood dripping on us, we will realize on a very deep level that we have no right to hold a grudge against another human being: "All have sinned and fall short of the glory of God" (Romans 3:23). That includes you and me. In order to hold on to an unforgiving spirit we must be blinded to the fact that we are as deeply in need of forgiveness as the one who harmed us. When we pretend we don't need forgiveness, we become self-righteous—no longer finding our righteousness in Christ.

Taking Action

1. Ask the Lord to show you the person you need to forgive as He sees him or her—a desperate soul in need of His love.

2. Many people who harm others have been deeply wounded in the past. Ask God to show you their bleeding hearts and help you be more compassionate.

3. Pray that the Lord will give you a clear and honest view of yourself without Him so you will understand your desperate need of His forgiveness.

4. Pray that the Lord will show you what sins you might have committed against others and your spouse.

5. Recognize that the desire to shy away from implementing these steps is normal. Human beings rarely enjoy having the light of God shine into the crevices of their souls to this level. But true forgiveness for others seldom occurs until we have encountered the truth of our own desperate need of forgiveness and the saving grace of Jesus.

Step 3: As much as lies within you, calmly and honestly share your pain with the person who injured you.

Instead, speaking the truth in love, we will in all things grow up into him who is the Head, that is, Christ. From him the whole body, joined and held together by every supporting ligament, grows and builds itself up in love, as each part does its work (Ephesians 4:15,16, emphasis added).

Honesty and openness especially apply to marriage. Otherwise the couple lives behind walls and never develops the intimacy God intends in marriage. Without honesty and openness, issues stack up, resentment festers, and the relationship wanes.

When abuses take place in a marriage, there is precious little choice but to be honest and express the pain. Peace in a marriage is never achieved by ignoring significant issues. I know some couples who have gone to the grave and never discussed "the affair" or whatever else happened in the past, so they never moved past the strain of the problem. A heavenly marriage is unattainable when shadowed by an unresolved past.

Taking Action

Talking about tough issues takes plenty of courage. The following suggestions should help. Remember, as the Lord leads, take one issue at a time unless several are interrelated.

1. Set an appointment to talk about the problem. If there is no physical or emotional danger, make sure you will have time and privacy. If you choose an unplanned discussion, use discretion regarding privacy and time.

2. Don't accuse and hurl insults; don't avoid the issues. Be firm and polite.

3. If appropriate, ask your spouse to pray aloud that you will be able to forgive him.

4. Expect tears. They're inevitable.

5. Once the issue has been discussed, don't keep bringing it up. Instead, exercise the truth found in Step 4.

6. Understand that two or three decades worth of unresolved conflicts may take several years to deal with.

7. Don't preach or evaluate your spouse's spiritual condition. Stick to the topic at hand.

8. If there is no remorse from your spouse, commit to praying about the issue and for your spouse. While someone asking our forgiveness can hasten the process and certainly facilitate reconciliation, true forgiveness does not hinge upon the perpetrator's remorse. It stems from *God's grace, mercy, and power.* This depth of supernatural forgiveness is available from the Lord even in the face of the abuser's disdain.

Personal Note

I have mixed thoughts about the necessity of confronting sexual abusers. Even though I know many professionals encourage this, I believe it might be better to not confront if he or she is someone you would rarely or never encounter. If the abuser is someone whom you see often, such as a family member, confrontation might be in order. *Use caution and plenty of wisdom.* Don't approach this person in private or alone. Some women have been raped again during confrontation. I have never confronted the person who sexually abused me—and I have no desire or need to. I have already experienced freedom and complete peace in Jesus.

Step 4: Commit to repeated mental forgiveness.

Then Peter came to Him and said, "Lord, how often shall my brother sin against me, and I forgive him? Up to seven times?" Jesus said to him, "I do not say to you, up to seven times, but up to seventy times seven" (Matthew 18:21,22 NKJV).

Traditionally, this passage is interpreted to mean that if someone sins against us 490 times we should forgive that person each and every time. Let me offer a new approach. Look at it this way: If someone sins against us, the negative incident will come back to us over and over again—perhaps 490 times—even after we make a decision to forgive. Remember how Erica said that after she decided to forgive her husband she had to continue to forgive him every day for quite awhile? (See chapter 7.) This mental visitation of the incident is what she was talking about.

Taking Action

Every time you think of the wrong done to you, "take captive every thought to make it obedient to Christ" (2 Corinthians 10:5).

1. Firmly tell yourself you have forgiven that person and the situation is now under the blood of Jesus. If you dwell on the sin, you will be tempted to fall back into bitterness.

2. If at all possible, think positive thoughts about the other person. For instance, Erica might think, "My husband is really handsome" or "He has always been a great father."

3. Train yourself to react in love rather than anger. When the irritation begins, go back to Step 1. Release that anger to the Lord and ask Him to replace it with joy and love. According to Les Parrott, "Plenty of research now shows that 'ventilation' techniques only reduce one's control against anger and encourage more frequent and aggressive forms of the behavior. When we practice letting angry feelings out, we become less able to control them the next time. Rather than 'ventilating' the emotion and getting rid of it, we find it returns more frequently. And, like a muscle that we exercise over and over again, those feelings we 'exercise' become stronger too."[3]

Step 5: Ask the Lord to give you a spirit of forgiveness.

> When they came to the place called the Skull, there they crucified him, along with the criminals—one on his right, the other on his left. Jesus said, "Father, forgive them, for they do not know what they are doing" (Luke 23:33,34).

If we are to live Christ, we must adopt a spirit of forgiveness that says there's nothing a person can do that I won't forgive. This type of spirit is from God and is the evidence that we have the mind of Christ (see 1 Corinthians 2:16). Jesus Christ exemplified the spirit of forgiveness when He died on the cross. Not only did He forgive our past and present sins, but He took care of all our future sins as well.

Forgiveness revolutionizes a marriage because it breeds security. My husband and I know there's nothing the other could do that we wouldn't forgive. Neither of us has to "walk on eggshells" around the other. I'm not going to pretend that if my husband had an affair I wouldn't struggle. I would. The pain would be great, and the journey to healing wouldn't be finished overnight. But I am committed to letting Christ's spirit of forgiveness in me prevail.

Taking Action

1. Pray not only that you can forgive the specific conflicts that are trapping you in bitterness, but also pray for a *spirit of forgiveness* that will empower you to forgive as future situations arise.

2. Ask your spouse to pray specifically that you will adopt a spirit of forgiveness.

3. Pray that your spouse will adopt a spirit of forgiveness.

4. Pray together as a couple that the Lord will immerse you in His forgiveness—together, for each other, for the past, and for anything that might arise in the future.

5. Realize that a spirit of forgiveness is rare, even around the church.

Reality Checks

Time

Don't expect to implement all the suggestions in this chapter in a few days. It may take weeks or even months to work through all the points.

General

While the process of romancing your husband sexually can certainly be initiated right away, the relationship issues could be a long-term project. As you continue to review each chapter and pray through the issues and points, you'll experience a closer walk with your husband and with God.

Spouse

Don't expect your husband to understand everything all the time. Conversely, don't expect to understand your husband all the time. Just this weekend, I lovingly looked at my husband and said, "I'm not trying to be insulting here...I really am interested in knowing...can you please explain why men enjoy using the remote to change the TV channel so much?" He said, "Because I want to make certain I don't miss something." I'm not sure I understand that one yet because doesn't switching channels constantly ensure that something will be missed? Be patient with your husband and with yourself as God revolutionizes your marriage in His time frame. Also be aware that the more hours a week you commit to sitting in the presence of God and seeking the Lord, the more He can and will work in your life and in your marriage.

Prayer Points for Romance

In your journey of forgiveness…

- ৬ Pray that the Lord will grant you and your spouse courage on the pathway of forgiveness.

- ৬ Pray that any sexual sins that overshadow your marriage will be completely forgiven and left in the past.

- ৬ If you were sexually abused, pray that you will receive the healing and extend the forgiveness necessary to remove the effects of that abuse in your life, your heart, and your marriage. Ask the Lord to remove any lingering pain and bitterness.

- ৬ If you and/or your husband had other sexual partners in the past, pray that God will remove the influence of those people from your marriage.

Romantic Notions

My dove in the clefts of the rock, in the hiding places on the mountainside, show me your face, let me hear your voice; for your voice is sweet, and your face is lovely.

Song of Songs 2:14

What I Did

I bought four romantic greeting cards and left them around the house in strategic places. That way, my husband would find them one at a time and be steadily reminded of my love.

My Reason

I was going out of town for a weekend speaking engagement, and I wanted my husband to feel appreciated, loved, and respected during my absence. When I'm away, Daniel manages the kids and household. He is an incredible man, and I wanted him to know just how much I appreciate his support and love, not only for me but for our children.

How I Felt

Satisfied and a little crafty. It was somewhat invigorating to leave a paper trail behind and to know that Daniel would stumble upon the cards one at a time.

The Obstacles I Overcame

I was racing around the house, trying to get out the door so I wouldn't miss the plane. Brooke, then four, was screaming for me to help her put on her underwear. I had precious little time to spare. Daniel was dashing in and out of the house, trying to get Brett off to school. I had to really be sneaky in order to leave the cards without being seen.

My Husband's Response

Later I called him from the airport, and he said with delight, "Hey, I found cards all over the place!" I laughed and he asked me how many there were. I told him four. He said he'd found all four, but that he had been on the lookout for more. Then he told me I was a really sweet woman and he really loved and appreciated me.

What I Wish I Had Done

I wish I had bought a few more cards. Four was a good number, but I think six would have been better.

Budget Suggestions

This cost from $1 to $2.50 per card. For pennies, you can create cards by hand or on your computer.

Special Note

A nice variation on this idea is to mail your husband cards; send him a card a day for a week. If you aren't going to be out of town but want to surprise him, mail cards to him at his place of employment.

9
Exciting Encounters

How handsome you are, my lover!
Oh, how charming! And our bed is verdant.
SONG OF SONGS 1:16

ARE YOU READY FOR EXCITING ENCOUNTERS and romantic notions? Some of the following ideas are from me and some are from friends. While reading these ideas, brainstorm ways you can adjust them to fit your unique taste and life.

The more you plan and scheme and devise ways to seduce your man, the more enthusiastic you'll become about your sex life. There have been several times when I wasn't in the mood in the least, but I knew my husband needed me. Therefore, I went ahead and plotted. By the time I got my plan laid out and in motion, I *was* in the mood. The more energy you put into seducing your husband, the more exciting it becomes for you. The more exciting it becomes for you, the more thrilled he will become. The more thrilled he is, the more exhilarated you will be. Soon, the two of you will become true lovers—not just two people living under the same roof—and every glance, every word will be laden with the nuance of expectancy. Your marriage will become a fulfillment of the Song of Songs. I am convinced this is God's perfect will for *every* Christian marriage. He didn't create sex to be endured; He created it to be a bonding experience that intertwines two souls in the essence of intimacy.

You don't need to incorporate these ideas every week. I plan something special for my man regularly, but not on a specific schedule. Sometimes two months slip by before I orchestrate another exciting scheme. But since I started romancing Daniel, our quality of intimacy has exploded, regardless of whether I have done anything special lately. The act of pouring energy into your sex life turns the flames of passion way up—and keeps them intense!

A suggestion that is a gentle marriage builder is marked with two interlocking hearts. If an encounter contains a heart with a flaming arrow, you might consider serving your man some heart medication before the encounter. If an idea has a "rocket" rating, you'd both better take some heart medication!

Creative Romance

1
Lingerie Scavenger Hunt

I will get up now and go about the
city, through its streets and squares;
I will search for
the one my heart loves.

SONG OF SONGS 3:2

What I Did

I took my husband on a lingerie scavenger hunt. I called his boss at work and
secretly arranged for him to have a day of
vacation on a Friday. I left lingerie in manila
envelopes at strategic places around town.
The first envelope was in his car. In the envelope was a piece of lingerie with a note that
told him where to go for the next stop and who
to talk to. Also on the note was a verse of a love

song. At each stop I did the same thing using the next verse of the
love song. One stop he made was at a small drugstore where I had
purchased some candy and left it in a gift bag, along with the
sealed envelope. The clerk handed him the bag when he asked for
it. She didn't know what was up or what was in the manila envelope. From there, my lover went to the post office and accessed
our box. An invitation to dinner awaited him (no lingerie this
time). From the post office, I planned one more stop for him to
pick up a prepaid movie rental and a bag of microwave popcorn,
but the movie store went out of business the day before so I had

to improvise. The last envelope was taped to our front door. I was waiting for him inside…dressed in milky-white lingerie.

My Reason

I thought this would be something really fun to build expectation and excitement.

How I Felt

Giddy. I really felt like I had pulled off the ultimate scheme on this one.

The Obstacles I Overcame

The day didn't go as planned at all. An elderly acquaintance died, and the funeral wound up being the same day. My husband and I were asked to sing at the funeral so I had to tell him I had secretively arranged for him to have the day off. At that point, he suspected something was up, but he didn't know what. After the funeral, I went through with the scavenger hunt as planned. The funeral put a damper on the day, but I was determined to not let anything destroy my plans.

My Husband's Response

After he went on the scavenger hunt, he came into the house opening the last envelope and smiling as if he'd won a million bucks. Later I took him out to eat at a Victorian mansion turned restaurant. He was smitten!

What I Wish I Had Done

Looking back, I wish I had rearranged the day for the following Friday. The funeral overshadowed our day. However, I was juggling children and my work, so I didn't have much choice. This event is a clear example that sometimes life just happens, and as wives with romantic missions, it is important to be flexible in the timing but firm in the plans.

Budget Suggestions

Including lunch, this event cost about $40. For the envelopes I used a three-piece lingerie set I already owned. I spent $15 on the new white lingerie I wore. If you already have some attractive pieces, there's no need to buy new ones. I spent $10 on his gift of chocolate turtles at the drugstore. Instead of buying a present, you could bake cookies and leave them at a strategic, safe place.

2

Reckless Love

*You have stolen my heart, my sister, my bride;
you have stolen my heart with one glance of your
eyes, with one jewel of your necklace....Your lips
drop sweetness as the honeycomb, my bride;
milk and honey are under your tongue. The
fragrance of your garments is like that of Lebanon.*
SONG OF SONGS 4:9,11

What I Did

My husband was relaxing on the couch when I dropped in front of him and repeatedly kissed the tops of his feet.

My Reason

I had just been on the phone with an individual who was having marital problems. During the conversation, I was overwhelmed with admiration, respect, and thankfulness that my husband has always put me and our children above any of his own aspirations.

How I Felt

A little surprised. I didn't plan on doing this at all, but as soon as I hung up the phone, the next thing I knew I was at his feet.

The Obstacles I Overcame

There was a chair between me and him that I had to climb over.

My Husband's Response

"What in the world are you doing?" I replied, "I'm kissing your feet because you have always put me and the children first. You have no idea how much I appreciate that." He said something like, "Well, that's enough. I don't want you kissing my feet." He shook his head and kind of smiled.

What I Wish I Had Done

Kissed his feet a long time ago.

Budget Suggestions

This one is free—unless you need to release some pride. If so, this will be one of the more expensive suggestions.

3
Hidden Dainties

I belong to my lover, and his desire is for me.
Song of Songs 7:10

What I Did

I hung a couple of my silky teddies in my mate's closet. We have separate closets, so this worked great. I just hung them in front of where his ties hang on the door. I did this about a year ago, and that's where the teddies are still hanging.

My Reason

I wanted to leave my tracks in his closet.

How I Felt

I snickered and really enjoyed the moment. I didn't say a word to him about what I was doing; I waited until he found them. During the wait, I almost burst with anticipation of his reaction.

The Obstacles I Overcame

I had to be sneaky. This happened on a Saturday, and he was lurking around the house.

My Husband's Response

He didn't say a word for hours and hours. I knew he must have been in his closet. As the afternoon wore on, he never once brought up the teddy escapade. Finally, I could stand it no longer and I dropped a hint. He asked me if I had looked into my closet. I raced to my closet, whipped open the door, turned on the light, and found a pair of his Hanes underwear hanging inside. I screamed with giggles, and he rolled with laughter.

What I Wish I Had Done

I should have known my husband well enough to figure he was up to mischief. I wish I had looked in my closet a lot sooner. I'm sure the agony of waiting all afternoon took a few years off my life.

Budget Suggestions

I already had the teddies so I didn't have to spend a dime.

4

Christmas Adventure

Come, my lover, let us go to the countryside,
let us spend the night in the villages. Let us go early
to the vineyards to see if the vines have budded, if their blossoms
have opened, and if the pomegranates are in bloom—there I will
give you my love.
SONG OF SONGS 7:11,12

What I Did

I arranged for a special date during the Christmas season, which also happened to be close to our anniversary. I saw a brochure advertising a "barge ride" on the city lake. The numerous barges loaded with passengers trolled around the lake for a tour of Christmas lights. On the shore, afterward, there was a bonfire, Christmas carolers, and a concession stand where popcorn, hot chocolate, and hot apple cider were sold. My husband and I went on Friday night. Since this was such a neat event, I also arranged for us to go back Saturday night with our children.

My Reason

I saw the brochure on a local merchant's counter. I thought this would be a nice event where we could snuggle and enjoy the scenery. It proved to be a wonderful time of bonding and joy. This was our anniversary weekend, and we weren't going to get to spend the night alone as we had in previous years. Therefore, I threw my heart into creating a magical weekend close to home.

How I Felt

This was one of those sparkling evenings I'll always remember. We were at peace and enjoyed the spectacular lights. I really felt the bond of being one with my husband and the joy of snuggling under his protective arm.

The Obstacles I Overcame

Usually around Christmas I'm facing a work deadline in early January. I was tired and under the pressure of being behind; nonetheless, I carved out enough time to create a romantic Christmas memory that will last a lifetime.

My Husband's Response

I told my husband I had some special events planned for the weekend and that everything was a secret. He tried to figure out exactly what I had planned. He knew we had to be there at a certain time. As he started getting ready and began shaving, he was shooting questions at me. I laughed and kept the mystery to myself. He finally guessed exactly where we were going. He thought he was really clever, and I was disappointed he had figured it out. I think I called him a turkey—in Christian love, of course! When we got to the lake, he was really impressed that I had planned the evening. After the barge ride, we huddled near the bonfire, held each other, and enjoyed the night.

What I Wish I Had Done

I wish I had connected with the chamber of commerce a long time ago. They have information on all sorts of local activities that make great dates. Also, the chambers in neighboring cities make excellent contacts for planning special days and/or evenings. Oh, and I wish I had brought a heavier blanket the first night. It was really cold on that lake.

Budget Suggestions

This barge ride cost $6 each. That, plus the snacks, totaled a whopping $18 for the entire evening. Since we ate dinner at home with the kids, there was no meal expense involved. My pastor's wife and I trade babysitting, so that was free. The only way to cut cost on this would have been if we brought our own popcorn and hot apple cider.

5

First Date

by Wanda E. Brunstetter

You are beautiful, my darling, as Tirzah,
lovely as Jerusalem, majestic as troops with banners.
Turn your eyes from me; they overwhelm me.
Your hair is like a flock of goats descending from Gilead. Your teeth
are like a flock of sheep coming up from the washing. Each has its
twin, not one of them is alone.
Your temples behind your veil are like the halves of a
pomegranate....My dove, my perfect one, is unique.

SONG OF SONGS 6:4-7,9

What I Did

It was 1965, and my husband was coming home from Germany after being stationed there. We'd been separated a long time, so I wanted to do something really special when he returned. On his second night home, I dropped our 16-month-old son off at my parents' house, put on my cutest pair of stretch pants and a frilly blouse, and drove my husband to the roller skating rink where we'd had our first date.

My Reason

The time we'd spent apart had been difficult and trying for both of us. I wanted to do something romantic that would help us get reacquainted.

How I Felt

I was nervous and excited, like a teenager on her first date. After all, I didn't know Richard much better than I had on that first date, a little more than two years before.

The Obstacles I Overcame

Finding a babysitter who would watch our son for free or almost free was my main concern. My parents generously agreed. Little Richie already knew them, so I felt comfortable leaving him there.

My Husband's Response

My husband was pleasantly surprised. He loved to roller skate. Flirting with me, as he'd done when we first met, seemed to come naturally. It was a fun evening with lots of talking, laughing, and getting reacquainted. We even shared a chocolate milkshake at the snack bar. Romance and a feeling of being on our very first date cascaded over us as we skated hand-in-hand to blaring music during "couples only." We were young and so much in love!

What I Wish I Had Done

It would have been wonderful if I'd had enough money to rent a hotel room for the night, but our budget was tight. We went home after our date to a quiet house. My folks must have known how important it was for us to be by ourselves, because they decided to keep our little guy overnight.

Budget Suggestions

The cost of gasoline to drive across town to the skating rink, the price of two admission tickets and skate rentals, and the milkshake made this recreation of our first date relatively cheap. Would I do it over again? You'd better believe I would![1]

6

Ordained Romance

*[Beloved:] Awake, north wind, and come,
south wind! Blow on my garden, that its fragrance may spread
abroad. Let my lover come into his garden and taste its choice
fruits.*

*[Lover:] I have come into my garden, my sister,
my bride; I have gathered my myrrh with my spice.
I have eaten my honeycomb and my honey;
I have drunk my wine and my milk.*

SONG OF SONGS 4:16–5:1

What I Did

In my husband's car I placed a gift bag that
contained sparkling grape juice (I love that
stuff), a slinky teddy, and a romantic card in
which I invited him to a special dinner. Then
I called him at work to alert him that there was
something special in his car. That afternoon I
broiled some steak, made broccoli and cheese,
and cooked potatoes. During our date, I was wearing an oversized
shirt—his favorite—and no slacks. I poured the sparkling grape
juice over ice as he waited at our formal dining table. I sat in his
lap and fed him his meal. Later in the evening, we curled up
together and watched a movie.

My Reason

During a time of prayer I asked the Lord to show me something I could do to make my husband feel really special. I had

never entertained the notion of feeding my husband until that moment. After thinking it over, I figured this would be a time of closeness and laughter.

How I Felt

I always feel a little smug when I come up with a new scheme. But this time I had to feel smug in the Lord since I really feel like this idea was God-inspired. What a blast—that we serve a God who wants us to experience such fun in our marriages!

The Obstacles I Overcame

My kids were home with me all day, and they kept asking me, "What's in the gift bag, Mamma?" They were in the van with me when I put the bag in my husband's car, and their curiosity raged. I told them it was a special gift from me to Dad and they would just have to accept that. Also, my husband decided to take off early from work and showed up at home an hour before I expected him. I had hoped to meet him alone, but the kids were still home. There was an awkward jumble of schedules during the time we were ushering the kids off with my friend.

My Husband's Response

By the time I pulled this one off, he was used to my romancing him. With a smile in his voice, he called home to confirm our date. After we enjoyed our sparkling grape juice, we settled at the table. I didn't tell him I was going to feed him until I began sitting in his lap. We both laughed and talked all during dinner. The whole event was quite intimate and bonding.

What I Wish I Had Done

A few years ago, my husband gave me a tape of love songs. I wish I had put the music on, but I totally forgot. However, *he* turned on some romantic music.

Budget Suggestions

I cooked the meal at home, so this was a low-cost event. The sparkling grape juice cost about $3. However, if you wanted to do something different, you could also have your meal catered.

7

Surprise Reminder

*How beautiful you are and how pleasing, O love,
with your delights! Your stature is like that of the palm, and your
breasts like clusters of fruit. I said, "I will climb the palm tree; I
will take hold of its fruit." May your breasts be like the clusters of
the vine, the fragrance of your breath like apples, and your mouth
like the best wine.*

Song of Songs 7:6-9

What I Did

I tied a sequined bra across Daniel's steering wheel while he was at work. I didn't leave a note or any other identification—just the bra.

My Reason

I wanted to let him know the fires were burning at home, and I was his all the way.

How I Felt

A little mischievous. I wish I had had a picture of his face when he opened his car door.

The Obstacles I Overcame

That day I was racing around trying to get the bra on the steering wheel before he went to lunch. The kids pulled me in several directions. Sometimes romancing my husband can become a major undertaking.

My Husband's Response

After lunch, he called me and just said, "Hey!" I burst into laughter. When he got home, I was on the phone. Grinning, he tried to put the bra on me over my clothes. I playfully knocked away his hands. When I hung up, he said, "Now, I want to see you wear it!" Later he admitted that he would have been extremely embarrassed if one of his coworkers had spotted the bra. He said they would have never let him live it down.

What I Wish I Had Done

I should have reserved this one for when my husband and his car were at home. That way, his potential for embarrassment would have been zero. I could also have put the bra in the glove compartment and left a note for him to check it out.

Budget Suggestions

I suggest you purchase a bra that's somehow different. A regular one doesn't quite cut it. You can purchase "special occasion" pieces at numerous places, from Wal-Mart to Victoria's Secret, and spend anywhere from $10 to $50 (or more).

8

Doorknob Switcharoo
by Gail Sattler

You are a garden locked up, my sister, my bride;
you are a spring enclosed, a sealed fountain. Your plants are an
orchard of pomegranates with choice fruits, with henna and nard,
nard and saffron, calamus and cinnamon, with every kind of
incense tree, with myrrh and aloes and all the finest spices. You are
a garden fountain, a well of flowing water streaming down from
Lebanon.

SONG OF SONGS 4:12-15

What I Did

I secretly swapped the doorknob from our master bath, which had a lock, with our bedroom doorknob, which didn't have a lock. I taped a movie for my kids and hid it. The next time my husband and I were "in the mood" in the middle of the day, I took out the movie and put it into the VCR. I set my kids in front of it, put the volume on *loud,* and pulled my husband into the bedroom. He was smiling, but knew the kids were all home so he was prepared for only a little tease. I pointed to the bedroom doorknob. He didn't understand until I told him I had switched the knobs. Now I had him! We were locked in—and the kids were locked out!

My Reason

A quiet moment during waking hours is almost impossible in a household of kids and pets. Sometimes when my husband and

I want a little romance, nighttime arrives and we're exhausted. Over the years this has happened too many times. Spontaneity is lost when you have children. Our kids are not old enough to be left alone, but they are old enough that they don't have to be watched every minute.

How I Felt

Sneaky—and that added to the thrill.

The Obstacles I Overcame

Guilt. I had locked the kids out, and if they wanted either of us we were busy. However, as adults, my husband and I have needs, too, and the kids can do without us for short periods of time. As it turned out, they didn't notice we were missing.

My Husband's Response

He was impressed by my ingenuity, and it touched him deeply that I would go to such lengths for a little afternoon delight.

What I Wish I Had Done

Thought of it sooner.

Budget Suggestions

This cost me nothing because I traded doorknobs. If you don't have a locking doorknob, go to the hardware store and get one. It's worth the hassle![2]

9

Doing Feet
by Lynette Gagnon Sowell

How beautiful your sandaled feet, O prince's daughter! Your graceful legs are like jewels, the work of a craftsman's hand. Your navel is a rounded goblet that never lacks blended wine. Your waist is a mound of wheat encircled by lilies. Your breasts are like two fawns, twins of a gazelle. Your neck is like an ivory tower. Your eyes are the pools of Heshbon by the gate of Bath Rabbim.

SONG OF SONGS 7:1-4

What I Did

My husband and I love giving each other foot massages. Our problem was that the relaxed one would have a hard time staying motivated to rub the other's feet. One night I suggested we try massaging each other's feet simultaneously. We sat at opposite ends of the couch facing each other and entwined our legs. Then I got out the body lotion and started rubbing one of his feet. I passed him the lotion bottle so he could massage one of my feet at the same time. Then, after about 15 minutes, we switched to the other foot.

My Reason

I thought it would be a fun way to minister to each other, talk, and relax. One of the things we determined from the start of our marriage was to stay best friends. Best friends enjoy talking and relaxing with each other. Massaging feet together is a way to have intimate contact and serve each other. We love it! A lady once asked me one of our marriage secrets. I simply replied, "Doing feet," then explained.

How I Felt

If there's one part of the body that tends to be unattractive, it's feet. The first time we gave each other foot rubs, I had to overlook his bunions and knobby toes as his foot rested on my stomach. But I also realized how much my husband loved me to care so tenderly for my ugly toes and calluses.

The Obstacles I Overcame

Seeing yucky-looking toes 18 inches from my face. Once I was concentrating on his relaxation and ensuring he enjoyed the foot rub, his toes didn't matter anymore.

My Husband's Response

My man always wants to try something different, so he liked the idea of turning our legs into a "pretzel" and massaging each other's feet. In fact, once the kids are in bed and it's our time, he's usually the first one to suggest "doing feet."

What I Wish I Had Done

Turned the phone ringer off. It's hard to get your legs untangled and hop on one foot across the room to the phone. I also think lighting candles, turning the television off, and turning on soft music would have made our first massage much more romantic. (By the way, from personal experience I recommend washing feet *before* giving a massage.)

Budget Suggestions

This costs a half an hour of time and some lotion. You don't need to use special foot cream. Regular lotion, limber fingers, and the time to talk is what pays off. Doing feet is a tradition we've kept for six years. We're still in love, still communicating, and our feet are happy, too.[3]

10

Grape Feast

Like an apple tree among the trees of the forest is my lover among the young men. I delight to sit in his shade, and his fruit is sweet to my taste. He has taken me to the banquet hall, and his banner over me is love. Strengthen me with raisins, refresh me with apples, for I am faint with love.

SONG OF SONGS 2:3-5

What I Did

My husband was leaning against the kitchen cabinet. Grapes were lying on the opposite counter. I spontaneously grabbed a grape, placed it between my teeth, and offered it to him. I repeated this gesture six times. (I remembered seeing Elizabeth Taylor do something like this one time, and I figured if it was good for Liz it was good for me.)

How I Felt

Sexy!

The Obstacles I Overcame

The fear of expressing my own sensuality. When we approach our husbands in this manner, we may be a little embarrassed—but that soon fades in the light of their reactions. Our two children were in the den watching television, so we had to be discreet!

My Husband's Response

With a smile, he ate half of the grape then followed with a rather expressive kiss. I continued placing grapes between my teeth and offering him bites. The kisses increased and got more intense. Finally he pulled back and said, "You are so sexy!"

What I Wish I Had Done

Bought more grapes!

Budget Suggestions

Buy seedless grapes—even if they are more expensive.

11

Dream Come True
by Wanda E. Brunstetter

All beautiful you are, my darling; there is no flaw in you. Come with me from Lebanon, my bride, come with me from Lebanon. Descend from the crest of Amana, from the top of Senir, the summit of Hermon, from the lions' dens and the mountain haunts of leopards.

SONG OF SONGS 4:7,8

What I Did

Since I was ten years old I've dreamed of riding in a sleigh. I thought it would be the most romantic thing on earth. Shortly after I got married, I began dropping little hints about wanting a sleigh ride. When I got no response, I came right out and announced, "I really want to go on a sleigh ride. Think how romantic it would be." Still nothing happened…not in 38 years! One day my daughter-in-law said, "Wanda, if you really want a sleigh ride, and you think it would be a romantic thing to do, then make it happen." I took her advice and called a little inn in the Bavarian village of Leavenworth, Washington, about two hours from our home. Part of their "romance package" was an hour-long sleigh ride.

My Reason

Being the more romantic one in the family, I decided to fulfill a lifelong dream and, at the same time, put a spark of romance back into our marriage. We would be celebrating our thirty-eighth wedding anniversary, and I was feeling as though we were beginning to take each other for granted.

How I Felt

I was excited, hopeful, yet a little nervous. I was bombarded by questions: What if Richard doesn't enjoy the sleigh ride as much as I do? What if he doesn't think it's romantic at all?

The Obstacles I Overcame

I had to do all the planning for this little getaway, persuade Richard to go, and juggle our bills so we could afford it.

My Husband's Response

Richard went along willingly, though it wasn't until we were actually on that sleigh, being pulled through glistening snow by two beautiful draft horses, that his romantic senses kicked in. "This is great, Honey," he whispered in my ear. "Let's come back again. In fact, maybe we could do this every year on our anniversary."

What I Wish I Had Done

My only regret is not having taken the initiative and planned a romantic sleigh ride for us sooner. Thirty-eight years was too long to wait!

Budget Suggestions

While probably not the cheapest romantic interlude, it was certainly worth the money. Total cost for a two-night stay, which included a full breakfast, gourmet dessert each night, coffee or tea served in the morning, and, of course the sleigh ride, was $280. Now I'm asking myself, "What else can I make happen? Maybe a hayride this summer?"[4]

12

Calendar Girl
by Carrie Turansky

*Where has your lover gone, most beautiful of women? Which way
did your lover turn, that we may
look for him with you?*

*My lover has gone down to his garden,
to the beds of spices, to browse in the gardens and
to gather lilies. I am my lover's and my lover is mine;
he browses among the lilies.*

SONG OF SONGS 6:1-3

What I Did

A short-term mission trip was going to
separate my husband and me for about eight
weeks. I'd be in Belgium, and he'd be at home
working. Mail was going to be unreliable and expensive, so I
decided to make a large poster-size calendar with a pocket for each
day I was going to be away. In the pockets I put a Bible verse, love
note, funny joke, or reminder of a special memory we shared.

My Reason

I wanted my husband to know I loved him even though we had
to be apart for a few weeks. I wanted him to have something from
me every day!

How I Felt

I had a lot of fun creating this special calendar just for my man.
While I was away it helped me deal with my own loneliness, too.

Knowing he had the calendar and a special note from me each day lifted my spirits and helped me feel more connected to him.

The Obstacles I Overcame

It took me several days to make the calendar, so it was tricky to keep it a secret.

My Husband's Response

He enjoyed the poster and appreciated all the work I put into it. Our love was even stronger when I returned. This daily reminder of our love helped keep us close even though we were continents apart. He kept the calendar for several years.

What I Wish I Had Done

I wish I would have taken copies of the notes and verses with me so I could read them on the same day he read them.

Budget Suggestions

Visit craft and art stores for great bargains. You could make your calendar very simple and use premade small envelopes, create your own little pockets, or go crazy and decorate each envelope with stickers and cut-out phrases and pictures from magazines or from your family album.[5]

Twelve Days of Christmas Poster

This variation on Carrie's idea will create a memorable Christmas your husband will love.

Make and decorate a Christmas poster. Use tinsel, bows, and even lights. Use your imagination! Each pouch will contain a special message along with a theme verse, either handwritten or typed, from the Song of Songs. Present this gift to your husband on December 14, so he will have a message a day until Christmas.

Tell him you are his "true love" and that the poster is his personalized Christmas calendar. The following suggestions coordinate with the symbols from "The Twelve Days of Christmas" song. Feel free to alter the suggestions to suit your husband's tastes and needs. Also, if your husband is as curious as mine, you might consider gluing the tops of the pouches together so they are tamper evident to encourage him to open them on the designated day.

December 14: A Partridge in a Pear Tree. Bake your husband a pear cake and hide it in the house. The pouch for December 14 will contain a note with a clue to the cake's whereabouts. Theme verse: Song of Songs 2:3.

December 15: Two Turtle Doves. Buy your husband some chocolate turtles or Dove chocolates and hide them in your lingerie drawer. Put a special greeting card in the poster pouch that tells him where he can find his treats. Theme verses: Song of Songs 5:10-16.

December 16: Three French Hens. Put a gift certificate good for one free lunch or dinner in the pouch. Take your husband to a restaurant where they serve great chicken or other kinds of fowl. If you're on a tight budget, cook him a special chicken dinner. Theme verses: Song of Songs 6:1-3.

December 17: Four Calling Birds. Buy your husband a prepaid phone card. Add a special note that tells him he can call his out-of-town relatives or a special friend. Theme verses: Song of Songs 8:6,7.

December 18: Five Golden Rings. Buy some gold garland. Cut five lengths, several inches long, and tape the ends of each one together. On notes, write down five reasons why you love your husband and/or five things that you admire about him. Tape the notes to the rings. Then place the rings in strategic places around the house or even in his car or workroom. Cut a tuft of the garland and tape it to the note you place in the poster pouch. On the note write, "Look for a trail of five golden rings." Theme verses: Song of Songs 3:6-11.

December 19: Six Geese a Laying. Get six plastic Easter eggs and spray paint them gold or silver. In each egg, place poetry and/or special memories from your years together—how you felt the first time you met or kissed, the joy of the birth/ adoption of your children, the excitement of your wedding day. Place the eggs on the branches of your Christmas tree. Put a note in the poster pouch explaining that the Christmas tree holds some special messages for him. Don't tell him about the eggs; see if he can figure out where the messages are. Once he figures out the first one, he'll discover the rest. Theme verses: Song of Songs 1:2-4.

December 20: Seven Swans a Swimming. Place a special "award certificate" in the poster pouch that offers your husband a bath or shower with you. You can redeem the certificate at your own home or rent a hotel room that has a Jacuzzi. Theme verses: Song of Songs 1:16.

December 21: Eight Maids a Milking. Make your husband some homemade ice cream in his favorite flavor. Have his favorite sundae topping on hand. Put a note in the pouch that announces a special dessert after dinner. (If you're short on time, you can buy his favorite ice cream; but, making it yourself speaks of your extra effort to please him.) Theme verse: Song of Songs 5:1.

December 22: Nine Ladies Dancing. Create a special invitation for a romantic, slow dance in your house. Make sure to include the time and place (what room in the house) in your invitation. If you have children, wait until the kids are asleep then put on your favorite CD and sway to the music. Theme verses: Song of Songs 7:9-13.

December 23: Ten Lords a Leaping. Write a sexy love story for you and your husband. (See "Fantasy" for ideas.) If you have children, arrange for a babysitter that evening. Make your husband promise that he'll wait until he gets to work to read the story, then watch him leap all the way home! Theme verses: Song of Songs 5:2-5.

December 24: Eleven Pipers Piping. Today's poster note will tell your husband to expect a mystery caller that evening. Ask a local musician to come to your house that night and play a few love songs or some Christmas music for your husband. If the climate permits, have the instrumentalist play the music outside, in caroler fashion. Usually a college or high school student(s) from church will give 15 minutes of their evening—even on Christmas Eve—to earn some extra cash. Or perhaps a family member could play for you. If you have the money, hire a local professional from the city orchestra. Theme verses: Song of Songs 8:10-12.

December 25: Twelve Drummers Drumming. Buy your husband a CD or cassette from his favorite artist and put it in the calendar. Theme verses: Song of Songs 2:8-13.

13

Fantasy
by Janelle Burnham Schneider

*Who is this coming up from the desert like a column of smoke, per-
fumed with myrrh and incense made from all the spices of the
merchant? Look! It is Solomon's carriage, escorted by sixty
warriors, the noblest of Israel, all of them wearing the sword, all
experienced in battle, each with his sword at his side, prepared for
the terrors of the night.*

SONG OF SONGS 3:6-8

What I Did

My husband is in the Canadian military.
As a result, we are often separated, sometimes for months at a time. One of my
biggest concerns during lengthy separations
is how to help him cope with the lack of
physical intimacy. Since I am a Christian
romance author, one day I decided to use my
writing skills to create a story just for him and
me. In the story, I detailed our physical union and
described what I could envision us doing if we were together.

My Reason

I wanted to maintain our sexual intimacy in spite of our separation. Because I know that our physical relationship communi-
cates my love for him in a way he understands most profoundly,
I wanted him to be able to "feel" that love even though we couldn't
physically touch one another.

How I Felt

I wasn't sure how he'd respond to my story—whether he'd think it was too explicit or too contrived. I also felt very vulnerable putting such an intimate part of our lives on paper.

The Obstacles I Overcame

My obstacles were primarily mental and emotional. I had to overcome some personal inhibitions by putting words to something so private. I was also concerned about him opening the letter in public. Though we had frequent e-mail communication, I didn't trust this to cyberspace. I wrote it in hard copy, then mailed it to him with a note on the envelope telling him to open it in private.

My Husband's Response

The day he received the letter, he told me by phone that he had been pleasantly surprised by what I had written. He hadn't expected me to be as graphic as I was, but he really enjoyed it. He also commented later that the story had really helped him feel connected to me physically and emotionally, in spite of the miles between us. He also asked, "When do I get the next installment?"

What I Wish I Had Done

This one was regret free. I've written him several of these stories, and he's kept them all. Now when he has to leave for more than a couple of weeks, I see the twinkle in his eye that tells me he's looking forward to the next chapter.

Budget Suggestions

The only real investment is time and creativity. Putting intimacy on paper was hard at first, but his enthusiastic response helped make it easier. As the letters became a "counted on" event,

I invested in some special flocked stickers. He knew when he saw a "fuzzy" sticker on the envelope that it was "special" and should be opened in private.[6]

What You Can Do!

Create your own story. Janelle has written the following story to help you create your own letter of love. You can duplicate the story and insert your name and your husband's name or alter it to fit your unique situation. For instance, if your husband hasn't been out of town, change the story so it fits his work schedule. If you like, keep writing where Janelle leaves off and really make your husband's day!

Anticipation

Anticipation sent shivers down her spine as she changed the sheets on the queen-sized bed she shared with her husband. He was due home in just two hours. Since his flight would arrive well after the children's bedtime, they'd agreed that he would get a taxi home. He had no idea that the children weren't even home. Her parents had graciously agreed to keep the children overnight. They were excited about the sleep-over and had begged to go immediately after school. So she'd been home alone all afternoon and evening, with only her plans for company. She paused for a moment to enjoy the rare silence around her and delight in her surprise plans.

The solitude gave her freedom to let her imagination soar with thoughts of what she and her lover would enjoy tonight. Though they'd been married for years, her body still tingled at the thought of his touch. Their time apart had been hard, but it had also been good for them. She longed for his physical expression with a passion she hadn't experienced since their children were born. Smoothing the fresh-smelling sheets into place, she plumped his pillow just the way he liked and tucked it under the bedspread.

Then she gathered candles from around the house and placed them throughout their bedroom.

Her next step was a long soak in the tub. Not only was the steaming water a rare luxury, but she knew he especially enjoyed the scent of her skin fresh from the bath. Though she took a book into the bathroom, it lay unopened on the floor. Her imagination was too full of him for fiction to hold any appeal. She envisioned his expression when he realized what she'd done, then imagined how his lips would feel upon hers. She closed her eyes and leaned back against the tub, losing herself in waves of fantasies.

The cooling water brought her back to reality. She stepped out of the tub, dried herself, then spread scented lotion over every inch of skin she could reach. For tonight, she wanted to be soft, relaxed, and sweet-smelling. Her household duties and mother-hood distractions had been laid aside. Losing herself in the delight of his return would be complete bliss. Nothing would rob her of the ecstasy of his warmth and love.

Back in her room, she opened the drawer of what he called "frillies" and selected the negligee in his favorite color. The last hour ticked by with agonizing slowness. She tried again to read, but her mind wouldn't stay focused on the story. So she padded through the house, closed the children's bedroom doors as if they were asleep, straightened couch cushions, and kept herself busy. At long last she saw the lights of the taxi coming up their street. She hurried to their bedroom and lit the candles.

Though she ached to greet him at the door, she forced herself to lay back against the pillows. The surprise would be better if he thought she was asleep in their room. The front door opened. His suitcase thumped against the floor. The locks clicked as he shut the door and snapped them into place. His footsteps neared the bed-room door, and she couldn't restrain herself any longer. She opened the door just as he reached it and threw herself into his arms.

Nothing in her imagination could equal being held close to his heart. He kissed her once in greeting, then again more deeply. His arms crushed her against him for several long moments before his hands moved up to cup the back of her neck as the kiss lengthened into rapture. The joy of holding him and being held by him made her want to laugh even while her body tingled, quivered, and heated with primal force. All of her senses focused on him— the feel of his hands moving up and down her body, the sound of his murmurs against her lips, the smell that was only him. The glow of desire in his eyes shone brightly.

Still locked in each others' arms, he backed her into their bedroom. "I'm home, my love," he whispered softly into her ear.

"Mmm hmm," she murmured against his neck, "and it's just us."

He inched away and looked into her eyes, a smile curving the lips she wanted to kiss again.

"Where are the children?"

"Mom and Dad have them for a sleep-over," she responded, putting a husky, sexy note into her voice. "Do you mind?"

"Oh no." He assured her with another deep kiss. "I never dreamed I'd have you all to myself when I finally got home." His ragged breathing matched hers.

She hugged him tighter. "I missed you so much."

"And I missed you," he replied as he slid the negligee straps down her arms. "It may take me all night to show you just how much."[7]

10

Fine-Tuning Your Heart

*As the deer pants for streams of water, so my soul pants
for you, O God. My soul thirsts for God, for the living
God. When can I go and meet with God?*

PSALM 42:1,2

BY THIS POINT, I hope you are already seeing a miracle occur in
your marriage. Truly God is in the business of transforming our
marriages into fulfilling, exhilarating journeys. As you celebrate
your exciting relationship or begin making it better, these devotions will help you focus on how to "wow" your husband and
create a union that makes every day a new adventure.

This chapter contains three weeks of devotionals. Use these
devotionals in your regular prayer time to deepen your understanding of God, your mate, and your unique relationship with
each other.

/

The Birds and the Bees

How beautiful you are, my darling!
Oh, how beautiful! Your eyes are doves.
SONG OF SONGS 1:15

Passage: Song of Songs 1:9-15

My sister-in-law, Jeanna, recently faced the task of detailing the birds and bees to her ten-year-old daughter, Brandi. She had brought home a note from school stating that they would be viewing a film about reproduction and the functions of the female body. Jeanna, being a conscientious mother, decided she should be the one to introduce the subject to her daughter. So she placed her two younger children in front of the television and took Brandi into the bedroom for "the talk."

"What do you know about this note, Brandi?" Jeanna asked, showing her the note from school.

"Nothing," Brandi answered, her candid blue eyes innocent.

"Do you understand anything this note says?" Jeanna asked gently.

"No. All I know is they're going to put all the girls in one room and all the boys in the other and show us a film," Brandi replied with a shrug.

Well, here we go, Jeanna thought with discomfort. Then she began informing Brandi of the wonderful experience of having a monthly cycle and explaining that this means her body is capable of becoming pregnant.

After some thought, Brandi asked, "So, does this mean that after your body starts this you can just get pregnant?"

Jeanna said, "No. It takes a man and a woman for a woman to become pregnant."

"Wait a minute," Brandi said, raising her hands for emphasis. "I have a question."

"Okay," Jeanna said calmly, although her discomfort steadily grew.

"Let's just say that a boy and a girl like each other a whole bunch, and they start kissing a whole bunch. Can a girl get pregnant then?"

"No," Jeanna explained, "you can't get pregnant from kissing. The way you get pregnant is…" She delicately informed Brandi of the details of the propagation of the human race.

In response, Brandi picked up her bed pillow and covered her face for several silent moments of embarrassed contemplation. Finally she removed the pillow and asked, "You mean *Dad did that to you?*"

"Yes," Jeanna said, desperately trying not to laugh.

"That's *disgusting.*"

"It can be," Jeanna said, her face impassive despite the hilarity about to burst forth.

"So, after that, then does your body just keep having babies?"

"No," Jeanna said, "every time you want a baby you have to do that."

Brandi, her ten-year-old mind whirling, said, "Wait a minute! You have *three* kids."

"Yes," Jeanna said.

"So that means Dad did that to you *three times!*"

"That's right," Jeanna said, on the brink of exploding with laughter.

How did you learn about sex? Fortunately, my mother was like my sister-in-law, conscientious enough to share the truth with me. But a "wiser and older" aunt, three years my senior, had already supplied me with many of the details. After the explosion of the sexual revolution, parents realized they needed to detail the facts at an earlier age than our grandparents would have ever imagined.

Clearly, the sexual revolution brought about many negative changes in our society, but there are a few positive results as well. For instance, it's now okay for Christians to talk about sex within the appropriate setting. And it's okay to explain the birds and the bees to our daughters and sons. We can avoid the unfortunate situation of sending our daughters into the first night of their marriage with little or no idea of what might befall them. It's also okay for a married woman to enjoy sex. We can avert an even more tragic situation that one of my elderly acquaintances once admitted: She was so indoctrinated with the evils of sex that she refused to disrobe during intercourse, even after years of marriage.

In the United States, Christians have finally arrived at the wise conclusion that God created sex and that He intended for married people to find fulfillment with each other. I believe that is a big part of the reason Song of Songs is in the Bible. Although this book serves as a metaphor for the relationship between us and the Lover of our souls—Jesus—it also serves as a statement that romance and sexuality are to be celebrated within marriage. Given the numerous Bible passages where God speaks against immorality, we might very easily be deceived into believing that God frowns on physical intimacy. But then there's Song of Songs to balance the scales and encourage us to enjoy pleasure with our spouses.

What is your attitude toward sexuality? How does it align with God's Word?

Lord, as I move closer to Your perfect will in my marriage, please remove any negative opinions I have about sex. Give me a new view of what You planned in the Garden of Eden. I know Adam and Eve weren't ashamed in their nakedness. Father, deliver me from any shame I feel about being sexual with my husband.

2

Take Initiative!

There is a time for everything,
and a season for every activity under heaven.
ECCLESIASTES 3:1

Passage: Ecclesiastes 3:1-8

Would you like to make your man feel like a million bucks? Then do your best to meet his sexual needs. According to Dr. Gary Rosberg, 50 to 90 percent of married men view their sexuality as a major element in their worth as a man.[1] Therefore, when a wife doesn't see the need to take any initiative in their sex life, a husband may interpret it as a lack of worth on his part. While I believe most men enjoy the chase, it never hurts for women to let them know they're available to be chased.

How often do you initiate sex? Maybe the time has come to start! Your husband will probably be delighted if you take an active interest in the romance of your marriage. I'm talking about being romantically assertive—not dominating. Most men don't like bossy women. (And most women don't like bossy men.) To avoid being bossy or annoyingly aggressive, see yourself as your husband's personal seductress. Instead of barking out, "Let's have sex," give him a wink and a crook of your finger...then see how long it takes him to catch you.

Lord, give me the insight to recognize my husband's needs, and grant me the courage to fulfill them. Deliver me from the bondage of embarrassment and help me see there's nothing sinful about initiating sex. Remind me that our need for physical intimacy exists because You designed us that way.

3

Why Can't We Be Friends?

I no longer call you servants...
Instead, I have called you friends.
JOHN 15:15

Passage: John 15:9-17

Every person alive craves the loyalty of a devoted friend. Jesus understood this and wrapped His arms around everyone. What a holy example of friendship! If we are to be Christlike, then we are to extend friendship not only to the person across the street, but also to our spouses. Jesus' main concern is that we remain in His love (John 15:9); and His main command is "love each other" (verse 17). Proverbs 17:17 says, "A friend loves at all times."

In order to become our husbands' friends, we must be willing to love at all times—even when we don't feel like it; even in the face of our husbands' imperfections. A true friend doesn't keep records of past wrongs, but pushes toward a positive present and future.

Become your spouse's best friend. Live friendship even when the positive emotions aren't there. A friend...

- ♭ is truthful

- ♭ is loyal

- ♭ is faithful

- ♭ avoids verbal and nonverbal infidelity

- ♭ applauds accomplishment

- ♭ understands needs

- ♭ shares common interests

- ♭ enjoys what a friend loves

When a man and wife are best friends, they would rather be with each other than with someone else. Pledge to strengthen your friendship with your husband. Focus on him as the most important human being in your life.

Father, I confess that I have spent more time being a friend to my girlfriends than being a friend to my husband. Please forgive me. Help me be my husband's best friend. Teach me to trust him, to love him, to laugh with him, and to share his hobbies and interests. Create such a bond between us that my husband becomes my favorite person.

4

It Takes Two to Tango

Do not deprive each other except by mutual consent
and for a time, so that you may devote yourselves to prayer. Then
come together again so that Satan will
not tempt you because of your lack of control.

1 CORINTHIANS 7:5

Passage: 1 Corinthians 7:3-5

Recently, I learned of a woman who only offered sex to her husband if he brought home so much money per week. If the guy missed the dollar mark, he didn't get sex that week. A well-meaning friend stated the obvious, "You're acting like a prostitute, not a wife."

Our society is so sexually focused that a man—even a godly man—who isn't sexually fulfilled by his wife will be sorely tempted to find satisfaction elsewhere. When a wife uses sex like a weapon instead of a free gift, she intensifies her husband's needs. Please don't misunderstand me. I am *not* saying that a sexually deprived man has the right to have an affair. Sin is sin, and God holds a person responsible for his actions. If a woman is purposefully withholding sex from her man, God will hold her responsible for violating this biblical command: "Do not deprive each other except by mutual consent." Paul cites spiritual issues as a reason, but there are other times a couple may choose to abstain, such as the time surrounding the birth of a child.

With these truths in mind, some affairs can be viewed as "couple sin." It usually takes two to tango, and that involves enabling sin as well. By the time an affair occurs, years of neglect have usually festered. The husband neglects the wife's need for affection. The wife neglects the husband's need for sex. The walls go up in the marriage, and each partner develops a me-focus. The selfish attitudes mount; the sin increases. One spouse has an affair, and the other one feels shocked and betrayed. I know there are some women who *do* meet their husbands' needs and they still have affairs. For instance, King David had numerous wives that did his bidding, yet he still took Bathsheba (see 2 Samuel 11–12). But this is usually not the case.

What attitudes do you have toward sex? Is it something you freely share with your husband or something you use to manipulate him? Are you willing to invest energy in romancing your husband before it's too late?

Father, teach me to view my body as not only mine, but also my husband's. Help me to celebrate sex with my husband. Give me a new sensitivity to my man's needs, and don't let a spirit of selfishness creep into my heart. Teach me to be a generous lover.

5

Mr. Wonderful

All night long on my bed
I looked for the one my heart loves.

SONG OF SONGS 3:1

Passage: Song of Songs 3

Have you ever thought, *I wish I had never even married my husband! I'm convinced I was out of God's will. I just know there was a better match out there for me.*

When a marriage hits some rough territory, many people may feel that way. It's easy to fall into the trap of believing another spouse would make the marital journey different. In truth, much of marriage is the same for most couples. Even if you married another spouse, chances are you'd wind up in a mundane marriage all over again. "Tired" marriages are inevitable if a wife (or husband) doesn't commit to stirring the embers on a regular basis. Since God admonishes us to keep our vows, why not put energy into this marriage?

When you married your husband, what traits did you find so fascinating on your wedding day? Revisit those traits. Focus on your husband's good points. Look at him with a fresh eye. Your dream man just might be sharing your bed already!

Dear Father, forgive me for not appreciating my husband. Give me a fresh look at my man. Remind me of all his good traits and teach me to focus on them rather than his faults. I desperately want to fall in love with my man all over again. Give me Your love for him.

6

I Wanna Hold Your Hand

His mouth is sweetness itself;
he is altogether lovely. This is my lover,
this my friend, O daughters of Jerusalem.
SONG OF SONGS 5:16

Passage: Song of Songs 5

How long has it been since you *really* held your husband's hand? Since you *truly felt* the texture of his palm against yours? Since you looked deeply into his eyes? When was the last time you let him know he isn't alone in this journey called life? How long has it been since you *radically lived out* unconditional love and ministered to him—whether that means sitting together or fulfilling a specific need?

It's so much easier to hear God "calling" us to a ministry at church than it is to hear His voice when He beckons us to minister to our own mates. Yes, the ministry is reciprocal. I'm not saying you are the only one who should minister. God calls *both* spouses to serve each other. But neither am I saying that if your husband isn't ministering to you you have the right not to minister to him. As a godly wife, you are called to live by the Word of God, regardless of what your mate chooses.

Dare to put the Word of God into radical effect in your life. Even if your husband is not a believer, you will be amazed at what will happen in your marriage. Eventually, the two of you just might be falling all over yourselves to serve the other again. Never underestimate the power of God to transform broken lives into a melody of holiness.

Lord, I need courage. I'm afraid that if I truly live Your Word, my husband will not follow through and I'll feel frustrated and defeated. I'm tempted to continue in the old patterns because they're comfortable. Give me the courage and wisdom to begin living Christ and ministering in my marriage.

7
Delightful Differences

*[Isaac] went out to the field one evening to meditate, and as he
looked up, he saw camels approaching. Rebekah also looked up and
saw Isaac. She got down from her camel and asked the servant,
"Who is that man in the field coming to meet us?" "He is my
master," the servant answered. So she took her veil and covered
herself. Then the servant told Isaac all he had done. Isaac brought
her into the tent of his mother Sarah, and he married Rebekah. So
she became his wife, and he loved her; and Isaac was comforted
after his mother's death.*

GENESIS 24:63-67

Passage: Genesis 24

Some researchers have put forth the theory that there are no
major differences between men and women. Quite frankly,
it's hard for me to believe that anyone has ever accepted this
as truth. In my estimation, there is very simple proof that
this sameness between men and women does not exist.

Lipstick.

That's right. Lipstick. There's not a healthy male alive who
wants to wear the stuff. And many psychiatrists say that a
sign of mental health in a woman is her desire to look feminine—whether through pretty hairstyles, ruffled blouses,
or a little lip rouge. Now, when men start wanting to wear
lipstick…well, enough said!

I'm sure you've recognized that you and your husband
are as different as a watermelon and a camel. I wonder how
long it took Isaac and Rebekah to figure out they had major
differences. I wonder if Isaac ever looked at Rebekah and
asked, "Why do you like to wear nose rings anyway?" Perhaps

Rebekah gazed at Isaac and thought, "All the man thinks about is sex! I barely knew him, when the next thing I knew we were married and in the tent!" On the other hand, I wish I could have been there the first time they saw each other. There was probably enough electricity between them to catch a whole forest on fire!

That's the point of the differences. Opposites attract. And there's nothing more opposite than a man and a woman. And, oh, the sparks that can fly because of those delightful differences! Next time you're tempted to look down at your man for being "typically male", appreciate him for his masculinity instead.

Lord, I think You probably get a chuckle or two out of watching my husband and me. And, well, there are days when I wonder if the man I married is from another planet. But, Father, help me remember I have just as many quirks as he does. Don't let me get so focused on my husband's shortcomings that I miss his good points. Teach me to love his masculinity and appreciate our differences.

8
Home Run!

"In your anger do not sin": Do not let the sun go down while you are still angry, and do not give the devil a foothold....Be kind and compassionate to one another,
forgiving each other, just as in Christ God forgave you.

EPHESIANS 4:26,27,32

Passage: Ephesians 4:17-32

My husband is coaching my son's Little League baseball team. They have graduated from T-ball to a pitching machine. One of the things my husband has commented about is how hard it is to communicate to the boys from the pitcher's mound. He stands on the mound and has to holler over the sounds of the crowd to make sure they hear him. One boy, "Bart," had been having trouble with not running all the way to first base. If he thought he was going to be out, he'd stop running. That mistake cost him a base hit.

The next time Bart got up to hit, Daniel said, "Now, Bart, when you hit the ball, I want you to run to first base and don't stop running. Got it?"

"Yes!" Bart called back with a nod.

"I mean, you run as hard as you can and don't you stop for anything. Understand?"

Bart nodded again.

Daniel positioned the ball on the pitching machine and pulled the lever. The ball hurled forward. Bart clobbered it and started running to first base. The ball rolled across the infield, and we all thought Bart would stop on first. He didn't! He just kept on running, despite the fact that a nearby player was picking up the ball and there were runners on second and third. When the runner on second base saw Bart running toward him, he knew he didn't have a choice but to run himself. The runner on third leaped into action. Meanwhile, the team members, in little boy fashion, had a "three stooges" moment with the ball. They dropped it. They overthrew it. They fumbled it. And while Bart kept running, the third-base runner ran home. The second-base runner was forced to run home as well because Bart wasn't stopping for anything. Bart touched the third-base bag with his cleat and raced all the way to home. The crowd was cheering like crazy, and Bart's short-range hit drove home three points that eventually helped his team win.

When Daniel told Bart to run to first and not stop, Bart thought Daniel meant to not stop at all! Even at first base! When Daniel said, "Don't stop for anything," Bart thought his coach was telling him to run around all the bases.

How many times have you miscommunicated in your marriage? After nearly 20 years of marriage, I've lost count. But just as Daniel's miscommunication to Bart wound up winning the game, so the Lord can turn our marital bungles into home runs *if* we'll let Him. For every argument my husband and I have resolved, we usually feel much closer when the "I'm sorrys" have been said. And then there's always the making up!

Dear Lord, teach me how to be a better communicator. Help me speak my heart to my husband. And teach me to actively listen to him by repeating his thoughts back to him so we stay on the same track. I don't want to be guilty of creating walls between my husband and me. Let our conversations be a safe haven of trust and love.

9
Law or Love?

Love is the fulfillment of the law.
ROMANS 13:10

Passage: Romans 13:8-14

Is your approach to marriage based on law or love? When we have a list of rules and regulations regarding marriage, there is often little room for exercising and appreciating individual strengths. As a result, it is possible to miss the whole point of a Christian marriage? Are we losing sight of "two people oozing Christ's unconditional love all over each other"?

If you have bought into the thought process that you are not responsible before God for any area of your marriage or household, you are probably expecting your husband to become a cross between a saint and Casanova. You are highly frustrated because you see a host of things your man could do to enrich your marriage—if he just would! And you stay irritated with him in your home because he never is quite where you expect him to be spiritually. If this describes your marriage, you may be convinced that a rule-based, checklist marriage is what God expects. But that's leagues removed from what the Lord wants for His children.

Be the woman God designed you to be! Don't believe for one second that passivity is God's will for you. You are a woman uniquely crafted in the image of God. Dare to be yourself and show your love to your husband as only you can!

*Lord, show me my marriage the way You see it. Give me
and my husband the wisdom to identify any teaching*

that has put our marriage in bondage. Teach me to appreciate my own unique traits. Remind me that my marriage can and will be excellent when I pour healthy energy into it. Give me the kind of love that reflects what You intended.

10

Master?

For this is the way the holy women of the past
who put their hope in God used to make themselves
beautiful. They were submissive to their own husbands, like Sarah,
who obeyed Abraham and called him
her master. You are her daughters if you do what
is right and do not give way to fear.

1 PETER 3:5,6

Passage: 1 Peter 3:1-7

As I chose this passage, I almost cringed. I have seen such passages repeatedly used to limit and degrade women. However, even though such passages are misused and misinterpreted, it doesn't mean we can ignore them. There is truth and beauty in all Scripture because it is God-breathed. If women explore the nuggets of wisdom found in the Bible, they'll realize several healthy, balanced, spiritual truths.

First, submission is a powerful source of influence with husbands, whether they are believers or not. While God calls everyone to a spirit of submission, remember we are not "off the hook" even if our husbands don't understand.

Second, godly women realize that true beauty comes from within, not from perfect hair or makeup or costly designer dresses. Women naturally want to be pretty, and there's nothing evil about making ourselves attractive. However, we should never base our self-worth on the outward appearance, but rather on who we are before Christ. Our inner relationship with the Lord only grows and makes our spirits increasingly beautiful.

I used to resist passages like today's because I've seen them so abused. But one day I decided to start calling my husband "master" and see what happened. By the time I got to the point of calling him this, I was so high from the effects of romancing him that I was game to try just about anything! I started saying things like, "So, how did your day go, Oh Great Master?" Or, "Sure, I'll pass the salt, Oh Great One." My husband just gave a goofy grin and rolled his eyes. Sometimes I'd throw in a flirtatious wink...you can fill in the blanks from there. Then one day he shocked me as he was leaving for work. He wrapped his arms around me and said, "I hope you have a good day...Oh Great One." The smile in his voice prompted a delighted giggle from me. Never once did I expect him to return my endearments. I was astounded and thrilled!

Which brings us to the third point from this Scripture. When we dare to look at the whole Bible for advice on marriage, we can no longer turn a blind eye to the passages that don't fit our preconceived ideas. "Husbands, *in the same way* be considerate as you live with your wives...." When Paul says "in the same way," he is referring to everything he has just told wives. Husbands are admonished to do everything for their wives that he has told the wives to do for them.

"So in everything, do to others what you would have them do to you" (Matthew 7:12).

Father, help my resistant spirit. Teach me to read the whole Bible, not just a few passages, for understanding. I want to radically apply every area of Your Word to my life and marriage. Help me see my husband as a "master," not a child.

A *"Chayil"* Woman

A wife of noble character who can find?
She is worth far more than rubies.
PROVERBS 31:10

Passage: Proverbs 31:10-31

Some people have bought into the myths that women are better than men and that to be of worth a woman needs to be an executive with a six-figure income. Parts of society have certainly fed women a mountain of untruths. Another lie that even the secular world is now refuting is that there are virtually no differences between men and women. I'm not sure why this latter assumption ever became public. There are probably a million differences between men and women! We think differently. We act differently. We process information differently. Our bodies are different. Our desires are different.

Unfortunately, in a knee-jerk reaction to some of society's erroneous views, many Christian women believe that the opposite of being "worldly" is passivity. In order to be pleasing to God they must make sure they are: 1) spiritually weaker than their husbands; 2) inactive in the spirituality of their households; 3) not taking initiative in other areas of their marriages (including sex). Paul's statement that "the husband is the head of the wife as Christ is the head of the church" (Ephesians 5:23) has been misrepresented to provide a framework for limiting husbands and wives, rather than empowering them.

In order to embrace the doctrine of female passivity, Christians must turn a blind eye to the powerful biblical women, including the Old Testament prophetess and judge, Deborah, Queen Esther, and the Proverbs 31 woman. In today's Scripture, "noble character" is from the Hebrew word *chayil*, which really means "might, strength, power, able, valiant, virtuous, valor, army, host, forces, riches, substance, wealth." Chayil is used 244 times in the Old Testament. For example, in Proverbs chayil is used when talking about the power of a godly woman in her home.

In the marriage relationship, men *and* women bring an element of God-ordained power that has nothing to do with control or chauvinism (female or male). Dare to ask the Lord to reveal His plans for you. You will soon discover that He cherishes you and adores you as a valuable creation. Take the time to read and reread stories of women whom God honored. Then realize that He honors *all* men and women who seek Him.

Lord, help me base my concepts of marriage on what the whole Bible says. Show me the wealth of Your blessing as presented throughout Your Word and the power of Your presence in my home and marriage. Teach me to view myself the way You view me. Deliver me from any insecurities I feel because I have been told I'm a lesser person in Your eyes through misinterpretations of Your Word. Remind me daily that I was created in Your image, and that You cherish me.

12

The Great Mender

The Spirit of the Sovereign LORD is on me,
because the LORD has anointed me to preach good
news to the poor. He has sent me to bind up the brokenhearted, to
proclaim freedom for the captives
and release from darkness for the prisoners.

ISAIAH 61:1

Passage: Isaiah 61

The other day my little girl sat near my feet while I was putting on my makeup. "Mamma," she asked, "can you make this bracelet into a necklace? I want to put it around my neck." I looked down to see that she had a small plastic bracelet that would never fit around her neck.

I replied, "Sugar, I can't do that. In the first place, it's not going to fit over your head. In the second place, to even try to slip it around your neck I would need to break it. That was not made to be a necklace; it was made to be a bracelet."

As I mused on this situation, I realized it paralleled many marriage experiences. God did not intend for a wife to be her husband's mother. A wife is to be her husband's lover, mate, friend, partner, and companion. When a woman becomes a mother-wife, she essentially breaks the marriage to fulfill a role God never intended. Like the bracelet would have never fit around Brooke's neck, such a marriage never seems to "fit" just right. This means couples can go through their whole lives and never once taste the ecstasy of what it means to set aside control and manipulation and become true lovers—to really become one and be a living example of God's unconditional love.

Is your marriage "broken"? God is in the business of mending broken relationships and turning them into something more precious than either you or your husband could ever imagine. Will you allow God to break the negative cycles in your life so your marriage can become a haven of heaven?

Father, I'm beginning to realize that I'm responsible for some of the problems in my marriage. Please give me the wisdom to move toward becoming a lover-wife. I'm not even sure I know how to be my husband's lover. But You made him, Lord. You know him better than I ever will, so begin showing me today what actions I can take that will enable You to strengthen my marriage.

13

A Spirit of Oneness

by Jeanette K. DeLoach[2]

The man and his wife were both naked,
and they felt no shame.

GENESIS 2:25

Passage: Genesis 2:4-25

Creating a spirit of oneness is important to sexual intimacy. If your marriage is not healthy, your sex life will suffer. Recognize that in marriage God has joined you together. It goes beyond any choice you made of a partner. Have a couple mindset. Take your husband into consideration when making your decisions. Doing so will show him that the things he does for you are recognized and that he is special. In a marriage relationship we are stewards of an intimacy God has blessed us with. Couples who realize they are one relish the mystery of this oneness. They use their marriage to honor God. In being pleased with one another, we are pleasing the Lord because He created this oneness.

Another important aspect in having a healthy marriage is an atmosphere of acceptance. One of the most wonderful gifts you can give your partner is accepting him for who he is. Most people try to change their mates into who they want them to be. That is just the opposite of acceptance and tears the relationship apart. Knowing one another's needs and wants is important to intimacy. Know each other well enough to share your thoughts, needs, hopes, and dreams. Resolve conflict before you engage in an intimate moment. Nothing kills the mood faster than harbored resentment.

There's no such thing as a great marriage without a great sex life. That is not defined by frequency or variety. A healthy sexual relationship is one in which *self* is left outside the bedroom door. Both the wife and husband should feel comfortable enough with each other outside the bedroom to be able to share their wants, needs, and desires with one another during intimacy. It should be a celebration of God's gift of sex. Sexuality is a way to express love and respect. It is a way to show our husbands that we appreciate them and what they do for us. If we are not putting everything we have into that, then we are depriving each other of the most wonderful gift, next to the product (children) of this intimacy, that God has given us. Make sure that the environment going in is free from criticism and manipulation.

Commitment is also very important to intimacy. The vows spoken before God were a covenant a promise not to be broken. For sexual intimacy to happen completely, both parties have to feel no fear of rejection or loss. Having the knowledge that they are both in it for the long haul leaves a feeling of security that can only increase intimacy and sexual fulfillment.

Dear Father, teach me to celebrate sex with my husband. Break the bondage of my past. Help me to move into a new realm in my marriage. Oh, Lord, don't let me live my whole life and never understand the powerful intimacy You can create between a husband and wife.

14

Space and Grace

When I was a child, I talked like a child,
I thought like a child, I reasoned like a child.
When I became a man, I put childish ways behind me.

1 CORINTHIANS 13:11

Passage: 1 Corinthians 12:31–13:13

My seven-year-old son knows how to iron his clothes, cook his breakfast, dress himself, tie his shoes, comb his hair, give himself a bath, water the garden and my plants, and take responsibility for his homework. My five-year-old daughter knows how to get on the kitchen stepladder and wash dishes, warm up her milk in the microwave, give herself a bath, dress herself, tie her shoes, do her hair, and paint her nails. (I'm always close by if they need help, though.) The last time my children's three cousins spent the night, I slept in while my seven-year-old son used the "Egg Wave" system to micro-wave egg omelets for himself, his three cousins, and his sister. My children have an allowance and are learning to manage their money—including paying their tithes. As I write this sentence, my children are, for the first time, taking the ini-tiative of putting a load of towels in the washer to wash them. Wow!

Do my children do these tasks perfectly? No. When my son irons his clothes he might miss a spot. My little girl gets as much fingernail polish on her fingers as she does on the nails. When she fixes her hair, strands are usually sticking out. She misses spots on the dishes that she washes, and she might not rinse off all the soap. My son usually leaves a mess in the kitchen when he makes microwave omelets—the package of shredded cheese might be sitting on the cabinet, an eggshell may be left on the floor. I won't be surprised if the load of towels includes a shirt or two. (Just as long as a cat doesn't get in, we're in good shape!) But I won't ever complain about any of these imperfections! My goal as a mother is to *enable* independence.

When I was seven, I ironed my clothes. When I was eight, I was learning how to cook. I paid my own expenses during my high school years, bought my own car, my own clothes, and paid for my senior ring. Recently I heard of a five-year-old who, in the good ol' days, got up every morning, built a fire, and cooked breakfast for the entire family. That included hand-rolled biscuits!

My point? *Helplessness is learned.* It is a taught cycle of behavior. If my children can do all they do for themselves at such a young age, then I have a strong hunch that healthy, grown men don't need their wives to be their mothers by picking up after them, nagging them, or re-doing the chores they volunteer to do. Are you willing to empower your man to be an adult? Even if it means letting him do things his way and to his standards? Be a lover-wife, not a mother-wife. Although this transition may take time—you won't regret it.

Father, I confess that, at times, I have been a mother-wife. Help me stop viewing my husband as helpless. As long as I think of him that way, I cannot truly respect him as an adult. Give me the grace to give him space. Give me the wisdom to accept what he's done and not try to fix it. Help me be his lover, not his mother.

15

A Temporary Storm

As a father has compassion on his children, so the LORD has
compassion on those who fear him; for he knows how we are
formed, he remembers that we are dust.

PSALM 103:13,14

Passage: Psalm 103

My husband and I don't argue much, but, like any other
married couple, there are tense moments. Such was the case
one particular evening. The issues we "discussed" don't need
to be detailed, but we did exchange a few firm words in front
of the children. While we don't exert major effort to hide
our small tiffs from our children, it is rare indeed that they
witness their mom and dad in an argument.

In the midst of our swift exchange, my son, Brett,
exclaimed, "Wait a minute! You're arguing! But I thought
you said you never argue!"

"No," I responded. "I never told you that Dad and I don't
ever argue. What I told you was that we almost never argue."

That ended the short-lived verbal exchange between my
husband and me, but a cloud of tension settled between
us—a cloud that tainted the rest of the evening. Daniel and
I avoided each other when at all possible. Neither of us spoke
to the other unless absolutely necessary. Frankly, I was wondering what planet he fell off of and thinking that if he
wanted *me* to romance *him* that night he was nuts! However, I suspect that he was wondering if I was from another
solar system altogether and pledging to avoid any and all
romantic musings.

Well, that "delightful" evening wore on until bedtime loomed in our faces. At last I noticed six-year-old Brett posting red, heart-shaped stickers along the dining room wall. Then he strategically put one on the corner of the dining table. Next, he placed stickers that led to my husband, sitting in the den. Then Brett said, "Mom, you start right here and follow the stickers." He pointed to the line along the wall in the dining room. Then he said, "Dad, you follow your trail of stickers." He pointed to the line of stickers along the wall that led to Daniel.

Like the good, obedient parents we are, we followed our designated assignments until we each stopped at the same spot near the dining room table.

"Now," Brett said, "you can make up."

Daniel and I shared a sheepish smile then embraced. The tension evaporated. We exchanged humble apologies. And I once again realized that my husband really was from planet Earth and that I was married to the most wonderful man alive.

No marriage, regardless of how stable, is free of bumps in the road. Les and Leslie Parrott, the gurus of marriage relationships state, "We still admit to impatient moments, angry impulses, jealous surges, and all the rest. We still have needs, drives, and goals that aren't easily harmonized with self-giving love."[2] All married couples have times when exhaustion and differences of opinion lead to tense moments. However, God's ideal for a Christian marriage is for a climate of love and cooperation to exude because our spirits have merged and we no longer consider our individual interests alone. I believe the Lord desires the overall tone of our marriage to be oneness and that His grace abounds during strained encounters. As today's verse reveals, God fully understands that there will be days when things don't operate smoothly in our marriages. Trust Him to help smooth out the rough places.

Father, help me not major on the minors. Remind me that I have idiosyncrasies like my husband does. Teach me to be as slow to anger as You are. Don't let me get so focused on my husband's faults that we stay in conflict. I don't want to miss out on experiencing a marvelous marriage.

16

My Grandmother Would Kill Me!

"For my thoughts are not your thoughts, neither are your ways my ways," declares the LORD. *"As the heavens are higher than the earth, so are my ways higher than your ways and my thoughts than your thoughts."*

ISAIAH 55:8,9

Passage: Isaiah 55

As I near the end of this book, I keep having one recurring thought, *If my grandmother were alive, she would kill me!* She would absolutely fall apart if she knew I was writing such a book. When she got married (early in the twentieth century), nobody talked about sex. Good girls didn't really enjoy sex—or certainly didn't admit it if they did. Mothers often told daughters that sex was a wifely duty to be endured. If daughters had questions they confided in mothers instead of talking about the issues with the people they were having sex with—their own husbands. After a year of marriage, husbands probably scratched their heads and began to wonder, *Is this as good as it gets?*

It's very easy to laugh at our grandparents' attitudes toward sex, but are we much better? Many times, I've witnessed young wives roll their eyes in disgust and say, "That's all he ever thinks about." Or some church women buy into the notion that sexual passivity is somehow what God expects from females. Some people have even been taught that Christian women should never be anything but responders, that they are to wait for their husbands to romance them. And many women are afraid of being ridiculed or put down if they take any initiative in the bedroom.

These attitudes land most modern marriages about where many of our grandparents' marriages were—a gradual acceptance that mediocre really is as good as it gets. There were always a few in every crowd—even 100 years ago—that seemed to transcend mediocrity. Precious few, indeed. But for the most part...yawn....

What's going on in your marriage? Are you yawning? If so, perhaps the time has come for you to make a list of the wrong concepts that have evolved through your cultural conditioning, erroneous teachings of the Word of God, or what's been passed down through the generations. Wad up the list. Burn it. Get out the Word of God, open up to Song of Songs, and ask the Lord to redefine your attitudes toward sex and toward your man.

Father, You know my man better than I ever will. Right now, I'm asking You to give me a fresh, sexy idea that is tailored specifically for him. I'm going to sit here and be silent until You inspire my mind with Your creativity. And, Lord, I don't ever want to yawn again!

17
Continual Storms

For God did not give us a spirit of timidity, but a spirit of power, of love and of self-discipline.
2 TIMOTHY 1:7

Passage: 2 Timothy 1

In east Texas we have our share of violent storms. Some of them produce tornadoes that annihilate entire cities. Any time dark clouds boil across the sky, most of us snap on the weather channel to see if we're supposed to be blown away. When I was in graduate school (in Texas), I shared a class with a young woman from California. She said that people were always asking her how she could peacefully live amid so many earthquakes. She said, "Earthquakes? Earthquakes are *nothing* compared to all these tornadoes! It's enough to make you go crazy! Seems like every other time a storm blows up the weatherman is tracking a tornado. You keep looking at the TV screen and thinking, *It's getting closer! It's getting closer! I'm going to die!*"

Some marriages have such a spirit. There's a perpetual dark cloud hanging over the union, and the husband and/or wife live in continual fear that another tornado is going to rage through. Everything said, every expression, every gesture, every action is tainted with an undercurrent of hostility. Some Christian marriages have a climate of turmoil and tension with occasional spurts of harmony. This harmony might briefly surface during special occasions then, in the face of individual power struggles, vanish as quickly as it appeared.

This cycle of struggle is not God's plan for Christian marriages. Jesus is in the business of empowering couples, pouring His love into their lives and underscoring the relationship with a stability that comes through self-discipline. The Lord wants our marriages to be glimpses of heaven. He wants husbands and wives to be best friends, lovers, soul mates, and a picture of His unconditional love. Imagine how our world would be impacted if Christian couples truly demonstrated Christ's unconditional love.

What is the weather like in your marriage?

Jesus, teach me to love the way You do.

18
A Divinely Ordained Purpose

by Jeanette K. DeLoach[4]

Come away, my lover, and be like a gazelle or like a young stag on the spice-laden mountains.

SONG OF SONGS 8:14

Passage: Song of Songs 8:10-14

Couples need to know that their relationships have a divinely ordained purpose. God gave sex to married couples as a gift. This gift is for creating life (Genesis 2:24); for intimate oneness (Ephesians 5:31,32); for a unique knowledge of one another (Genesis 4:1); for pleasure (Proverbs 5:15, 18,19); and for comfort (2 Samuel 12:24).

How can we, as Christian women, show our husbands how much we love, respect, and desire them?

Be comfortable with yourself and your spiritual walk. This is key to being able to give all you have to your husband. Know you are a child of God. Know you are fearfully and wonderfully made.

Let go of past hurts. Being able to forgive your husband for things he has done in the past can only strengthen your relationship with him and with God. If you do not forgive, the Lord will not forgive you (see Matthew 6:14,15).

Do not compare yourself with other women. God made you just the way He felt you should be. If you are throwing yourself into taking care of your husband's needs, you have nothing to fear. Your husband will find you to be the most beautiful woman in the world if you give yourself to him without inhibitions. Take care of him. Show him you appreciate what he does for you.

Be willing to be vulnerable. You are only going to get as good as you give. If you are not putting everything you have into your intimate moments with your husband, they will never be the blessing the Lord says they can be. Remember that marriage is honorable and the bed should be kept pure (Hebrews 13:4). If God did not intend intimacy for good, He would have made it boring!

Every man is different. What pleases your man? Find out. When he says you look pretty, make a mental note of what you are wearing, how your makeup is done, and what you were doing at the moment. Some men find it sexually attractive to watch their wives go about their domestic duties or even to help in the process. Knowing his wife is working for him and their children pleases a man.

Make sure you respect your husband enough to give him your best. Think of pleasing him as you would please Christ. Prepare his favorite dishes. Wear the clothes he likes. Greet him at the end of the day with a smile, a long hug, and a slow kiss.

In recognizing that intimacy is a gift from God and that He intended for it to be good, we can let go of our inhibitions and misconceptions. Pleasing our husbands will please us. Pray about it *before* you approach your husband, and then give him all you have. You might be surprised at how good it can be!

Dear Lord, teach me how to give all I have. You made me a sexual being, so teach me how to be sexy. Deliver me from my inhibitions. Show me how to "wow" my man.

19

Dare to Fly!

Father, forgive them,
for they do not know what they are doing.
Luke 23:34

Passage: Luke 22–24

During the writing of this book, my little boy caught a monarch butterfly and released him in my office. When you have a five- and a seven-year-old on the loose you never know what kind of critters you'll encounter from one day to the next. Well, the monarch flew around awhile then started hanging here, there, and everywhere. Last night, he landed on my computer desk, near my left arm. I managed to catch him and walked to the outside door, opened it, and tossed the butterfly out. Well, the crazy thing turned around and flew right back in quicker than I could even attempt to catch him. The last time I saw him, he was hanging from the ceiling.

Sometimes I wonder if we're like that butterfly. God so desperately wants to free us from our past. As a matter of fact, He was so emphatic that He broke into time and came in the form of a human being, stretched Himself out on the cross, and offered Himself as the supreme sacrifice for our sins. Jesus Christ not only died on the cross to forgive you of your sins and purify your heart but He also died to deliver you from the heartache of the sins others have committed against you.

However, we can never experience healing unless we have first trod the pathway of forgiveness. Who do you need to forgive? Your mate? Your parents? A former mate? An abuser?

Give the pain to Jesus. He wants to scoop you into His arms and whisk you to freedom. Don't swoop back into the captivity of bitterness. Dare to fly! Fly for Jesus!

Father, I'm really struggling with forgiveness. Remind me just how much I need Your forgiveness. Oh, Lord, deliver me from the bitterness. I'm tired of that trap! Wrap Your arms around me and take me to freedom. Give me the gift of Your forgiveness—and the spirit of forgiveness. Forgive through me!

20

A Desolate Woman

*Tamar put ashes on her head and tore
the ornamented robe she was wearing. She put her
hand on her head and went away, weeping aloud
as she went....And Tamar lived in her brother
Absalom's house, a desolate woman.*

2 SAMUEL 13:19,20

Passage: 2 Samuel 13; Luke 7:36-48

Recently I spoke with someone who had been sexually abused when she was eight. It took place at the hand of a 12-year-old cousin. The woman was now in her 50s and just beginning to struggle with getting over being abused. She confided that a couple of years before she had finally broken the torment of silence and decided to counsel with her pastor. Her pastor essentially told her that boys would be boys and that she needed to get over it. Others said it was time for her to get on with her life.

The problem with these uninformed opinions is that after we've bottled up the pain from sexual abuse, when we open it the pain is still new. The act of bottling up the hurt and anger keeps the emotions so fresh that it's like the trauma has just happened. Once we start talking about the situation, the abuse might as well have happened the day before—even if the actual event(s) occurred 50 years earlier.

When a woman is sexually abused she becomes like Tamar—a desolate woman. Many women, like the dear one just mentioned, spend most of their lives living in that state. When a woman's virginity is robbed, she is forced to release a piece of her soul. If this is you, don't despair. God sees your loss. He not only sees your loss, He feels your loss. You might angrily think, *Why didn't God stop what happened to me? Where was He?* And I will answer without reserve…He was there. He was with you. When you were molested or raped, He felt every agony you endured. He wept with you, and He still weeps with you. He hasn't deserted you and He never did.

I'm not sure I can answer the whys, but I do know that the deeper the heart is wounded, the deeper the love of God must go. Allow God's love to plunge to the depths of your sorrow. Don't hold Him at arm's length. Begin the healing process. Buy some worship music, plop onto your couch, close your eyes, and listen. Simply "be still, and know that [he is] God" (Psalm 46:10). The healing will not be fast, and it won't be cheap. Commit to 30 minutes to one hour a day of doing nothing but absorbing the presence of the Lord. And in the midst of soaking Him up, ask Him to remove the effects of the abuse from you. Jesus is the Divine Healer. You don't have to stay desolate your whole life.

It's been 22 years since my sexual abuse. With every year that slips by, I feel the Lord taking my healing to a deeper level. I'm still praying, and I know the Lord will complete my healing. In fact, I feel as if that process is close to completion. I'm living proof that God wants to heal and is eager to heal all those who *will ask* and *take the time to embrace the healing.* You don't have to stay a prisoner of the past. You can stand victorious in Christ—a new creature empowered to impact your world, your marriage, and your household for the Lord.

Your husband needs you to be his lover. You cannot fully meet that need until you recover from the past. Let the recovery begin today.

Oh, Father, I'm desolate...so desolate. I feel as if I'm a shriveled prune inside. There's no life within me. I know I need to be a good wife, but sex is so painful. All it does is bring back bad memories. Lord, I don't want the memories anymore! Heal my mind. Heal my emotions. Heal my soul. Remove the effects of that person from me. Help me step forth to embrace the future, to be a new creature in You.

21
The Whole Truth
and Nothing but the Truth

*They will turn their ears away from the truth
and turn aside to myths.*

2 TIMOTHY 4:4

Passage: 2 Timothy 4:1-8

Have you read through the Bible from Genesis to Revelation? If so, how many times? If not, perhaps it's time to start. The Bible is chockful of marriage-changing truths that so few people tap into. Often what happens is that people pick out four or five passages from the Bible and build their marriage concepts while ignoring the rest of the Bible. For instance, it's easy to take the famous Ephesians 5 passage on submission and erect a system of rules and regulations for the marriage that completely ignores key concepts such as Matthew 7:12: "So in everything, do to others what you would have them do to you, for this sums up the Law and the Prophets." Another passage that brings balance to any marriage is: "Also a dispute arose among them as to which of them was considered to be greatest. Jesus said to them, 'The kings of the Gentiles lord it over them; and those who exercise authority over them call themselves Benefactors. But you are not to be like that. Instead, the greatest among you should be like the youngest, and the one who rules like the one who serves'" (Luke 22:24-26).

It's very easy for Christians to be deceived and believe that error is truth or half-truth because many aren't actively interacting with the *whole* Bible on a regular basis. Begin reading the Word of God for yourself—not just one verse a day or by using a snatch-and-grab system. Methodically read and study the Bible over and over again. With every chapter, ask yourself, "Is there anything God is showing me that will strengthen my marriage?"

Start with Song of Songs (to spice up your marriage, of course), then go to Esther, Ruth, Psalms, and the four Gospels—Matthew, Mark, Luke, and John. Remember, truly biblical marriages fall within the context of Christ's message of mutual submission and selfless love. Buy some reputable Bible commentaries and for every verse you read consult them. Make sure the commentaries take the entire Word of God into account. The only way to really tell if the commentary is isolating Scriptures to prove a predetermined concept is to know your Bible well enough to spot errors or questionable views. Two Bible commentaries that have a generally healthy view of men and women in relationships are *Adam Clark's Commentary on the Whole Bible* and *The Victor Background Bible Commentary* (Victor Books). Also, the *Reflecting God Study Bible* (Zondervan/Beacon Hill Press) is an excellent source for a balanced view on all subjects. Find out for yourself what the Greek and Hebrew words mean by buying a Hebrew/Greek study Bible or consulting *Strong's Exhaustive Concordance of the Bible*.

Dare to spend hours a week in the Word of God! If that means you have to get up at 4:00 A.M., so be it. If that means you have to stop watching your favorite TV program, so be it. The God who created the universe has given you the key to a heavenly marriage. As you apply the truths, not only will you begin to grow closer to God, you will soon find that your marriage will become a thriving love affair!

Father, in the past I have not studied Your Word like I know I should. Give me the willpower and discipline to begin reading the complete Bible. When I hear people instructing on marriage, give me the courage to dig through Your Word and find out if they are representing the whole truth or just a partial truth. Keep me humble, Lord. Prevent me from becoming arrogant in my search for truth. Don't allow me to be deceived into believing that a mundane, law-based marriage is Your perfect will. Show me a new vision of what You want my marriage to be. Show me the power of Your Word as I radically apply it to my life. Give me the fortitude to not turn a blind eye to the passages that make me uncomfortable. As I learn Your Word, bring to mind key verses that will bring balance and keep me from interpreting Scripture to mean something that contradicts Your radical message of love, dying to self, and putting others ahead of myself. Thank You for loving and watching over me.

Notes

Chapter 1: "The Queen of Romance"
1. Taken from 1999 statistics found at the National Center for Health Statistics website, National Vital Statistics, vol. 48, no. 19.
2. Gary Smalley with John Trent, *Love Is a Decision* (Dallas: Word Publishing, 1989), p. 51.
3. Willard F. Harley, Jr., *His Needs, Her Needs* (Grand Rapids, MI: Revell, 1986), pp. 12-13.
4. Gary Rosberg and Barbara Rosberg, *The Five Love Needs of Men and Women* (Wheaton, IL: Tyndale House Publishers, 2000), p. 8.
5. Harley, *His Needs, Her Needs*, p. 41.
6. Ibid., p. 43.
7. Ibid.

Chapter 2: A More Excellent Way
1. Lawrence O. Richards, *The Victor Bible Background Commentary: New Testament* (Colorado Springs: Victor Books, 1994), p. 484.
2. James Dobson, *Romantic Love* (Ventura, CA: Regal Books, 1989), pp. 23-25.

Chapter 3: Space and Grace
1. Author unknown.
2. Les Parrott and Leslie Parrott, *Like a Kiss on the Lips* (Grand Rapids, MI: Zondervan, 1997), p. 40.

Chapter 4: Love's Secret
1. H. Norman Wright, *Communication: Key to Your Marriage* (Ventura, CA: Regal, 1974), p. 24.
2. Stan Toler, D.Min., interview, April 6, 2001.
3. Quest Study Bible, Marshall Shelley, et al., eds. (Grand Rapids, MI: Zondervan, 1994), p. 1687.
4. Lawrence O. Richards, *The Victor Bible Background Commentary: New Testament* (Colorado Springs: Victor Books, 1994), p. 484.
5. Joseph Coleson, "Gender Equality: The Biblical Imperative," *Preacher's Magazine*, March/April/May 2000, vol. 75, no. 3, pp. 4-8. Dr. Coleson is a pastor and a professor of Old Testament at Nazarene Theological Seminary, Wheaton, IL.
6. Reflecting God Study Bible, Ken Barker, et al., eds. (Grand Rapids, MI: Zondervan, 2000), p. 9.
7. Quoted in Wright, Communication, p. 10.
8. Gary Rosberg and Barbara Rosberg, *The Five Love Needs of Men and Women* (Wheaton, IL: Tyndale House Publishers, 2000), p. 8.
9. Linda Dillow, *Creative Counterpart* (Nashville: Thomas Nelson, 1986), p. 142.
10. Mother Teresa, *A Simple Path*, Lucinda Vardney, comp. (New York: Ballantine, 1995), p. 99.

Chapter 5: Communication and Sex
1. H. Norman Wright, *Communication: Key to Your Marriage* (Ventura, CA: Regal, 1974), p. 54.
2. Gary Rosberg and Barbara Rosberg, *The Five Love Needs of Men and Women* (Wheaton, IL: Tyndale House Publishers, 2000), p. 65.
3. Pamela Lister, "10 Things Your Man Really Wants in Bed," *Redbook*, June 2001, p. 124.
4. Ibid.
5. Rosberg and Rosberg, *Five Love Needs*, p. 69.
6. Ibid., p. 68.
7. Doug Rosenau and Catherine Rosenau, "Real-Life Soul Mates," as quoted in Gary Rosberg and Barbara Rosberg, *Becoming Soul Mates* (Grand Rapids, MI: Zondervan, 1995), p. 155.
8. Jack O. Balswick and Judith K. Balswick, *The Family: A Christian Perspective on the Contemporary Home*, 2nd ed. (Grand Rapids, MI: Baker Book House, 1999), pp. 223-24.

9. Paul Hegstrom, *Angry Men and the Women Who Love Them* (Kansas City, MO: Beacon Hill Press, 1999), p. 107.

10. Questions 1–7 are taken from Linda Dillow, *Creative Counterpart* (Nashville: Thomas Nelson, 1986), p. 113.

Chapter 6: The Controlling Factor

1. William L. Coleman, "Spousehold Hints…His…Hers," *Moody Monthly,* February 1973, p. 47.

2. Laura Doyle, *The Surrendered Wife* (New York: Simon and Schuster, 2001), p. 53.

3. Ibid., pp. 47, 57.

4. Bryan Chapell, *Each for the Other: Marriage as It's Meant to Be* (Grand Rapids, MI: Baker Book House, 1998), p. 118.

5. Ibid., p. 121.

6. Aida Besancon Spencer, *Beyond the Curse: Women Called to Ministry* (Nashville: Thomas Nelson, 1985), p. 17.

7. Laurie Hall, *The Cleavers Don't Live Here Anymore* (Ann Arbor, MI: Servant Publications, 2000), p. 135.

8. Les Parrott and Leslie Parrott, *Like a Kiss on the Lips: Meditations on Proverbs for Couples* (Grand Rapids, MI: Zondervan Publishing House, 1997), p. 40.

Chapter 7: Surviving the Storms

1. Paul Hegstrom, *Angry Men and the Women Who Love Them* (Kansas City, MO: Beacon Hill Press, 1999), p. 28.

2. Gary Rosberg and Barbara Rosberg, *The Five Love Needs of Men and Women* (Wheaton, IL: Tyndale House Publishers, 2000), p. 8.

Chapter 8: Pathway of Forgiveness

1. Mother Teresa, *A Simple Path,* Lucinda Vardney, comp. (New York: Ballantine Books, 1995), p. 85.

2. For potent help on overcoming sexual abuse and past pain, see the devotionals in chapter 10 titled "Dare to Fly" and "A Desolate Woman." Also my book *The Harder I Laugh, The Deeper I Hurt* (with Stan Toler) and my novel *For Your Heart Only* show a realistic portrayal of the pain and healing from sexual abuse. *Healing for Damaged Emotions* and *Putting Away Childish Things,* both by David Seamands, are "must" studies for anyone with a past of sexual abuse.

3. Les Parrott and Leslie Parrott, *Like a Kiss on the Lips* (Grand Rapids, MI: Zondervan, 1997), pp. 69-70.

Chapter 9: Exciting Encounters

1. Wanda E. Brunstetter, "First Date," used by permission.

2. Gail Sattler, "Doorknob Switcharoo," used by permission.

3. Lynette Gagnon Sowell, "Doing Feet," used by permission.

4. Wanda E. Brunstetter, "Dream Come True," used by permission.

5. Carrie Turansky, "Calendar Girl," used by permission.

6. Janelle Burnham Schneider, "Fantasy," used by permission.

7. Ibid.

Chapter 10: Fine-Tuning Your Heart

1. Gary Rosberg and Barbara Rosberg, *The Five Love Needs of Men and Women* (Wheaton, IL: Tyndale House, 2000), pp. 57-58.

2. Jeanette K. DeLoach, "A Spirit of Oneness," used by permission.

3. Les Parrott and Leslie Parrott, *Love Is: Meditations for Couples on 1 Corinthians 13* (Grand Rapids, MI: Zondervan, 1999), p. 96.

4. Jeanette K. DeLoach, "A Divinely Ordained Purpose," used by permission.